Advance Praise for *Elegant Simplicity*

A wonderful manifesto for a life well-lived...like its author, this book is wise, warm, and simply elegant.

— David Orr, Paul Sears Distinguished Professor of
Environmental Studies and Politics Emeritus, Oberlin College

Satish Kumar's book *Elegant Simplicity* is the distillation of his lifetime of ideas and actions. It shows the intimate connections between the inner and outer world, soil, soul and society, beauty, joy and non-violence. It indicates that solutions to the big problems of our time—climate change, hate and violence, hopelessness, and despair—lie in thinking and living with elegant simplicity, reducing our ecological footprint while enlarging our hearts and minds.

— Vandana Shiva, activist and author,
Earth Democracy and *Who Really Feeds the World*

Satish Kumar embodies the elegance of simplicity in his life and his teachings. I have learnt both wisdom and creative solutions from him to complex problems. Follow his path to make your life simple elegant and inspiring.

— Deepak Chopra

An inspiring explanation of the fruits of simplicity and what living simply involves, by a writer who has experienced what it means to live a simple life.

— Mark Tully, former Bureau Chief of the BBC, New Delhi,
journalist and author, *No Full Stops in India*

In *Elegant Simplicity*, Satish Kumar shares extraordinary insights from his incredible life of spiritual activism, teaching, and practical living. A profound and accessible guide to an ecological civilization of peace, material sufficiency, and spiritual abundance for all. A must-read for all who seek an alternative to an economy now driving us to self-extinction.

— David Korten, author, *When Corporations Rule the World,
The Great Turning*, and *Change the Story, Change the Future*

There is no one on the planet better-equipped to tackle this project, and his insights will make you think and rethink how you're living and how you might change. Powerful!

— Bill McKibben, author,
Falter: Has the Human Game Begun to Play Itself Out?

My parents married during the Great Depression, which shaped their values that were passed on to me: "Live within your means," "Save some for tomorrow," "Share, don't be greedy," and "Work hard for the necessities in life, but money does not make you a better or more important person." Those life lessons were swept aside as post-war America chose consumption as the way to economic recovery. When the economy becomes society's goal rather than a means to a higher end, Donald Trump is the ultimate consequence. In this moving and eloquent book, Satish Kumar takes us through his own journey to a simpler, happier life with a low ecological footprint. In a time of lavish consumerism, loneliness, and alienation, Kumar's message is an uplifting gift that is a welcome antidote.

— David Suzuki, award-winning geneticist, author,
broadcaster, and environmental activist

Reading Satish Kumar's books is always uplifting! In *Elegant Simplicity* he distills a life of commitment to positive action and experience into his deep love for the human family and all life on this beautiful, endangered planet. He honors us all at the deepest level by acknowledging the abundance we create when we trust and care for all in our biosphere , practice forgiveness, and enjoy all the simple delights of everyday life. Beyond all sects and ideologies, this book is a benediction!

— Hazel Henderson, author, *Creating Alternative Futures*,
and founder & CEO, Ethical Markets Media

Weaving vivid stories and lucid wisdom teachings, gentle yet direct, this book is a magnificent embodiment of its title.

— Charles Eisenstein, author, *Climate: A New Story*

elegant simplicity

the art of living well

satish | kumar

new society
PUBLISHERS

Cover design by Diane McIntosh.
Cover Image: Breath © Olivia Fraser, www.oliviafraser.com

Printed in Canada. First printing March 2019.

Inquiries regarding requests to reprint all or part of *Elegant Simplicity* should
be addressed to New Society Publishers at the address below. To order directly
from the publishers, please call toll-free (North America) 1-800-567-6772, or
order online at www.newsociety.com

Any other inquiries can be directed by mail to:

New Society Publishers
P.O. Box 189, Gabriola Island, BC V0R 1X0, Canada
(250) 247-9737

LIBRARY AND ARCHIVES CANADA CATALOGUING IN PUBLICATION

Kumar, Satish, 1936–, author
Elegant simplicity : the art of living well / Satish Kumar.

Issued in print and electronic formats.
ISBN 978-0-86571-910-1 (hardcover).—ISBN 978-1-55092-703-0 (PDF).—
ISBN 978-1-77142-299-4 (EPUB)

1. Simplicity. 2. Conduct of life. 3. Sustainable living. 4. Social
values. 5. Self-actualization (Psychology). I. Title.

BJ1496.K86 2019   646.7   C2018-906384-X
                                                        C2018-906385-8

Funded by the Government of Canada · Financé par le gouvernement du Canada | Canada

New Society Publishers' mission is to publish books that contribute in
fundamental ways to building an ecologically sustainable and just society,
and to do so with the least possible impact on the environment,
in a manner that models this vision.

new society PUBLISHERS

Certified (B) Corporation

FSC · MIX · Paper from responsible sources · FSC® C016245

In dwelling, live close to the ground.

In thinking, keep to the simple.

In conflict, be fair and generous.

In governing, don't try to control.

In work, do what you enjoy.

In family life, be completely present.

— Lao Tzu

Contents

Gratitude and Thanks

This book would not have been possible without the help of many friends and associates.

First and foremost I would like to express my deep gratitude to June, my wife and life companion of 45 years. Over many months and with great patience and diligence, she has edited and corrected my manuscripts. Many of the thoughts and themes in this book have emerged out of our conversations over the years. Thank you June.

This book is truly a family affair, my daughter Maya has also put a tremendous amount of time and effort into reading, entering edits, and making practical as well as philosophical improvements to this book. Thank you Maya.

I have received huge help from my colleague Lynn Batten at the Resurgence Trust in correcting and improving copy again and again with painstaking accuracy. Thank you Lynn.

My gratitude goes out to Elaine Green, for her gracious and skillful support over the years. Elaine's constant and regular help has been invaluable. Thank you Elaine.

My colleague at Schumacher College, William Thomas, has been helpful and attentive in recording my Fireside Chats. Some of these conversations have been used in this book. These informal chats have also been transcribed by

Lee Cooper, who found time for this project in spite of his busy rehearsal schedule and many other commitments. Thank you William and Lee.

I am enormously indebted to Monica Perdoni whose thoughtful advice and deep insights have greatly contributed to the shaping of this book. Thank you Monica.

Last but not least, I have greatly enjoyed working with New Society Publishers. Thank you, Rob West and your entire team for your prompt and efficient handling of all matters relating to this book.

— Satish Kumar

Foreword

by Fritjof Capra

Satish Kumar has led an extraordinary life. Born in a small town in Rajasthan, India, he left his family home at the age of just nine to join the wandering Jains. He tells us that he was motivated to do so when, devastated by the sudden death of his father, he met a Jain monk who told him that by renouncing the world and following the way of the monks he could free himself from death and attain nirvana.

For the following nine years, the young Satish lived the rigorous life of a Jain monk, walking every day, never bathing, fasting frequently, and spending long hours in daily meditation. Then, at the age of eighteen, he secretly read in a book by Mahatma Gandhi that spirituality could be practiced by serving the world rather than renouncing it. Satish was so inspired by Gandhi's teaching that he left the Jain order and joined the Gandhian ashram of Vinoba Bhave, a close friend of Gandhi.

With Vinoba, Satish walked hundreds of miles campaigning for land reform in India. "As a monk," he writes, "I learned the art of walking, fasting, thinking, and meditating. At the ashram in Bodhgaya, I learned the art of making: cooking, gardening, and spinning cotton into yarn to make my own clothes. With Vinoba I learned how to meditate and with a friend decided to go on a pilgrimage for peace, inspired by the British philosopher and peace activist Bertrand Russell." Starting from Gandhi's grave in New Delhi, he and a fellow monk walked to Moscow, Paris, London, and Washington, D.C.—the capitals of the four nuclear powers. Carrying no money and depending on the kindness and hospitality of strangers, they were on the road for over two years, walking over 8,000 miles.

In 1973, Satish Kumar settled in the United Kingdom, taking up the post as editor of *Resurgence* magazine. In this capacity, he published a series of articles by E. F. Schumacher, the celebrated author of *Small Is Beautiful*, and over the years, he turned *Resurgence* into one of the most important and most beautiful ecological magazines. During the same time, Satish (as he is known to his friends and disciples around the world) inspired, originated, and directed a series of ecologically oriented projects, all of them tremendously successful. They include The Small School for the community of Hartland in North Devon, where he lives; the annual series of Schumacher Lectures; and Schumacher College, the celebrated center for ecological studies in South Devon.

I have been privileged to know Satish as a friend and colleague for over 30 years, and I have often wondered about the secret of his success in so many ventures. I think Satish gives us an answer in this book. *Elegant Simplicity* is his meditation on the nature of spirituality, seen through the lens of simplicity and based on his rich, lifelong experiences as a monk, Gandhian activist, eco-philosopher, educator, and spiritual teacher.

In the beautiful, eloquent, and passionate language that is characteristic of his speaking and writing, Satish weaves together the various threads that constitute a spiritual life of inner and outer simplicity. Simplicity, for Satish, like nonviolence for Gandhi, does not mean inaction. "Simple living is skillful living," he explains. Nor does it mean a loss of comfort: "Living simply and without clutter does not mean that we do not have a comfortable life. There is an innate elegance in minimizing possessions and maximizing comfort. Clutter brings chaos, simplicity brings clarity."

He points out that clutter brings chaos not only in our individual lives but also in the world at large: "Opulent living produces waste, pollution, and poverty." Thus, simplicity becomes a statement of social justice. Quoting Gandhi, Satish urges us to "live simply so that others may simply live." To achieve a state of elegant simplicity, he advises us to cultivate the simplicity of spirit, the simplicity of mind. "Simplicity of thought and mind," he writes, "will lead to a reduction of the desire for material things." And he concludes: "It may seem paradoxical but the gift of simplicity is the gift of abundance."

These passages resonate strongly with the Buddhist practice of mindfulness; and, indeed, Satish states explicitly: "Simplicity is a mindful way of living." I also noticed a Taoist flavor a few pages later when I read: "Simplicity is to flow through life as a river flows through a landscape."

In the subsequent chapters, Satish elaborates on these thoughts by discussing various aspects of a spiritual life embodying elegant simplicity. To begin with, he points out that moving toward simplicity represents a shift of emphasis from the quantity of material possessions to the quality of life, from finding shallow happiness in the acquisition of material objects to finding true fulfillment in human relationships and in relationships with nature. I have argued elsewhere that such a shift from quantity to quality will be essential for building an economy that is ecologically sustainable and socially just, and so I was not surprised to read Satish's assertion: "The way to sustainability is simplicity."

The question naturally arises: how do we get there? How do we achieve this goal of elegant simplicity? Satish's answer is that there is no formula or technique for simplicity. "Day after day," he advises us, "focus on simplicity of mind, thought, speech, feeling, action, food, clothes, house, intention, and relationships." This is a lifelong process with no final destination, he points out. And, not surprisingly, he concludes: "We are on a journey, a pilgrimage.... For me, elegant simplicity is rooted in the idea of pilgrimage. To be a pilgrim is to cultivate both outer simplicity and inner simplicity."

This insight leads Satish to offer us some deep reflections on the nature of pilgrimage, drawn from his extensive experience. On a pilgrimage, he tells us, there is very little planning. "Not being fixed and dogmatic with plans has its own magic, its own energy. When we allow things to emerge, miracles can happen."

At a deeper level, Satish continues, "the true meaning of pilgrimage is to live free from any attachments, habits, prejudices." Thus, for Satish, "pilgrimage is as much a metaphor as it is a literal reality. To be a pilgrim is to live lightly and simply in all circumstances, to embrace both delights and difficulties when they present themselves. Although I have made pilgrimages to holy places and sacred shrines of religious and natural significance, the deeper truth is that life itself is a pilgrimage."

Satish also associates his understanding of pilgrimage with the Hindu concept of karma yoga, which forms the very core of India's favorite religious text, the Bhagavad Gita. The philosophy of karma yoga, he explains, instructs us to act without desiring the fruit of our action. "Life is an eternal journey," he writes, "without a goal, without destination. Therefore we shouldn't focus on the outcome of our action; we should focus on the action itself."

An essential ingredient of elegant simplicity, according to Satish, is the art of making. "In my worldview," he explains, "a life of elegant simplicity would be built on the firm foundation of the arts and crafts. We need to move away from automation, industrialization, and robotic systems. We need to embrace the idea of mindful making."

For Satish, to be an artist is to be a maker. "Art is not a profession," he suggests. "It is a form of right livelihood where profession and vocation merge." He points out that "in indigenous cultures, art is neither a hobby nor a luxury, but rather an essential ingredient of everyday living and being." He envisages a society of cooperatives in which "employees and consumers are transformed into makers and artists." And finally, he asserts that "mindful making is like meditation. The mind has to be fully present in the moment of making."

This vision of artists and makers was the inspiration behind The Small School, a secondary school Satish created in his local community in Devon. Here is how he describes the school's curriculum: "We said, 'We are not going to teach only Shakespeare, Darwin, Newton, and Galileo; we are going to teach cooking, gardening, building, sewing, mending, woodwork, photography, and music in addition to maths, science, and English.' This was our curriculum. Our school was not going to be an exam factory; it was to be a place of self-discovery."

A few years later, Satish applied this profound idea of a school as a place of self-discovery to higher education with the creation of Schumacher College. I am fortunate to have taught courses there for more than 20 years, and I know the College very well. Schumacher College is a unique institution of learning. It is not a traditional college with a well-defined faculty and student body, and unlike most colleges and universities, it was not founded by any government agency, nor any individual or foundation associated with business. The College grew out of the global civil society that emerged during the 1990s. Thus, from the beginning, its faculty has been part of an international network of scholars and activists, a network of friends and colleagues Satish had built and nurtured as the editor of *Resurgence*.

Before the foundation of Schumacher College in 1991, there was no center of learning where ecology could be studied in a rigorous, in-depth way from many different perspectives. During the subsequent years, the situation changed significantly when a global coalition of NGOs was formed. This global civil society developed a network of scholars, research institutes, think tanks, and centers of learning that largely operate outside our leading academic institutions, business organizations, and government agencies. Today, there are dozens of these institutions of research and learning in all parts of the world. Schumacher College was one of the first and continues to play a leading role.

From the very beginning, Satish had the vision that the College should not represent a Eurocentric view but should give voice to a broad range of opinions, that it should be international. When Americans and Europeans discuss science, technology, and philosophy here, they are also joined by voices from Africa, India, Japan, and from other parts of the world.

The same ethnic, cultural, and intellectual diversity exists among the students. It has not been unusual for me to have 24 course participants (the limit that was established) from ten or more different countries. Participants are usually highly educated. They are professionals in various fields; some of them are young students, but there are also older people; and thus they contribute to the discussions from a multitude of perspectives.

Another key characteristic of Schumacher College is the strong sense of community it engenders. Participants come here for several weeks to live together, to learn together, and also to work together to sustain the learning community. They are divided into working groups that cook, clean, garden—doing all the work that is needed to maintain the College and fulfilling Satish's vision of "education with hands, hearts, and heads."

In these groups, conversations go on virtually round the clock. While they are cutting vegetables in the kitchen, people talk; while they are mopping the floor, or rearranging chairs for a special event, they talk. Everybody here is immersed in a continual experience of community and in exciting intellectual dialogues and discussions.

All this stimulates tremendous creativity. At Schumacher College, many things are created collectively, from meals in the kitchen to ideas in the classroom. Creativity flourishes because there is total trust in the community. To the faculty who teach at the College, it feels almost like being among family, and this strong feeling of community emerges after being together for not more than a week or two. To most scholars, such a situation is extremely attractive, as it offers us a unique opportunity to examine our work in depth, and to try out new ideas in a safe environment. Hence, Schumacher College is not only a unique place for course participants to learn in, but also for the teaching faculty to deeply engage over a relatively long period with a group of highly educated and highly motivated students, and to pursue a process of sustained self-exploration.

During the decades Satish served as the College's program director, he was the heart and soul of the Schumacher community. He cooked with the course participants, led morning meditations, taught courses, and shared his wisdom in a series of regular "fireside chats." Schumacher College is an embodiment of his vision of a community in which learning is integrated with mindful making, with meditation, and with elegant simplicity.

For Satish, meaningful education helps us overcome the concept of a disconnected self and fosters the awareness and practice of right relationships. "Training in elegant simplicity," he notes, "has to be rooted in the soil of right relationships." This is completely consistent with the change of paradigms that we are now experiencing in science and in society—a shift from seeing the world as a machine to understanding it as a network, from quantity to quality, from products to relationships. Satish characterizes this shift as one from *ego* to *eco*. "If we do not wish to complicate our lives," he writes, "then we have to shift from ego to eco. Ego separates and eco connects. Ego complicates, eco simplifies. *Eco* means 'home' where relationships are nurtured."

In the last chapter of the book, Satish summarizes his message by saying that we need to pay attention to three areas of existence: Soil, Soul, and Society. For me, these areas correspond to the ecological, cognitive, and social dimensions of life. "Soil," Satish explains, "is a metaphor for all environmental and natural relationships. Everything comes from the soil. Forests, food, houses, clothes come from the soil. Our bodies come from the soil and return to the soil. Soil is the source of life."

We need to value and replenish the soil, Satish reminds us. And he continues: "Similarly we need to replenish our soul.... We need to find ways of replenishing and healing the soul, the psyche.... Meditation is one such technique.... In meditation the outer world and the inner world meet. Soil and soul unite." And finally, "The wellbeing of soil and soul must extend to the wellbeing of society. This is possible only when we organize our society on the principles of human dignity, equality, and social justice."

To some, Satish's grand vision may sound overly idealistic. He is well aware of that, and he has a powerful reply: "You might call me an idealist. Yes, I am an idealist. But I ask you, 'What have the realists achieved? Wars? Poverty? Climate change?' The realists have ruled the world for far too long.... Let us give the idealists a chance."

The elegant simplicity Satish describes and advocates is also reflected in his language. He uses simple but powerful metaphors, and he always speaks from the heart. Reading his text almost feels like meditative practice. As I immersed myself in it, I experienced a feeling of great calmness and serenity. In all the years I have known Satish, I have always felt good in his presence, and I had the same feeling of well-being while reading this wonderful book.

— Fritjof Capra

Preface:
Let's Be Simple

"'Tis the gift to be simple,
'Tis the gift to be free..."

Thus begins a Shaker song written in 1848 by Elder Joseph Brackett. Shakers are the supreme example of elegant simplicity, the embodiment of beauty in simplicity. For the Shakers, minimalism is a way of life. For a long time, they have been my inspiration.

In my own life, the seeds of simplicity were sown when I became a Jain monk at the age of nine. The religion of the Jains is somewhat similar to the way of the Shakers. For Jains, a minimum of material possessions is a prerequisite for a maximum spiritual life. The more time you spend looking after worldly goods, the less time you have for meditation, for study of the scriptures, and for chanting and singing sacred mantras. Such was the teaching of my Jain Guru.

At the age of 18, I came across the writings of Mahatma Gandhi, another great champion of simplicity similar to the Shakers and the Jains. "Simple living and high thinking" was his motto. He lived in a simple hut which he had built himself, he spun the yarn for his loin cloth and his shawl. He grew vegetables and cooked his own food while leading the Independence Movement of India and editing a weekly journal. Thus he proved that it is possible to meet our physical needs through living simply and at the same time be socially, politically, and intellectually active.

For Gandhi, simplicity was also a statement of social justice. He subscribed to the ideal that you should "live simply so that others may simply live." An acquisitive and consumerist lifestyle necessitates the exploitation of the weak and of Nature. As consumers, we squander resources and waste our time and effort in chasing after things we do not need. We put greed above need, glamor above grace, and exploitation above conservation. Opulent living produces waste, pollution, and poverty.

My life both as a Jain monk and in a Gandhian ashram was one of utter simplicity. Thus the ideal of simple living became my second nature.

In 1962, at age 26, I decided to go on a pilgrimage for peace. I wanted to speak to the people and politicians of the four countries that possessed nuclear weapons. I said to myself, what can be more complicated, stupid, and cruel than the invention and possession of such weapons of mass destruction. I decided that the antidote to this most complicated weapons system was to undertake a pilgrimage of protest with the simplest of methods: a walk to the nuclear capitals of the world.

So I walked from the grave of Mahatma Gandhi in New Delhi, to Moscow, Paris, London, and Washington, D.C. It was an eight-thousand-mile pilgrimage. To make the journey even simpler, I walked (with my friend E. P. Menon) without a penny in my pocket. No money, no food, and on foot. We were on the road for about eight hundred days. These were the simplest and best eight hundred days of my life, and they changed my whole view of existence.

I became utterly convinced that to live a good, imaginative, and inspiring life we need very little in the way of manufactured material possessions. We can live by the sun, soil, and water, which are all gifts of the benevolent universe. We can live by mutuality and reciprocity, which are gifts of humanity. We can live by our hands, our legs, and our labor, none of which need to be bought from a supermarket or department store.

Living by love and generosity begets love and generosity. To live simply is to live in freedom and to trust that "all will be well and all manner of things will be well," as St. Julian of Norwich said. Simplicity brings us closer to the sublime truth, sustained goodness, and subtle beauty.

Living simply is neither laziness nor inaction. Actually, it is our consumer lifestyle which makes us lazy, deskilled, and inactive. We become dependent on mechanization, industrialization, and mass production. The ideal of elegant simplicity is connected with the arts and crafts, with the process of making, and with the art of living well on less. Simplicity focuses on the quality of life rather than the quantity of material possessions. *Being* rather than *having*, as Eric Fromm puts it.

When I live a life of simplicity, I celebrate the intrinsic value of making and let go of focusing on results or outcomes, achievements or accomplishments. Through arts and crafts, I am able to meet my needs and avoid being a victim of my greed. By being a maker, a creator, and a producer, I am able to find a sense of joy, fulfillment, and pleasure.

Simple living is its own reward. It is also skillful living—learning not only to use our heads and hands, but also to cultivate our heart qualities of love, forgiveness, and the understanding of the unity of all life. As Lao Tzu said, "simplicity, patience, and compassion are our greatest treasures."

Simplicity doesn't stop at minimizing our material possessions. We also need to cultivate simplicity of spirit. It is easier to give up our material clutter than to shed our psychological baggage. Pride, ego, fear, and anger clutter our souls and minds in the same way that piles of clothes, furniture, and other belongings clutter our homes. Therefore Shaker, Jain, and Gandhian views of simplicity are much more profound and deep than just ridding ourselves of material possessions and downsizing.

This book presents a comprehensive and all-embracing ideal of simplicity. Here I am exploring the ideal of elegant simplicity on the metaphysical as well as the physical level. Simplicity of being is as essential as simplicity of living. This is why I have included chapters on right relationship and limitless love. Straightforward and authentic relationships embedded in the ground of true love eliminate confusion and conflict among family, friends, and neighbors. If we happen to get into hateful and hurtful situations, then it is simpler to forgive and forget than carry the burden of resentment and revenge.

We complicate our lives when we are caught in the duality of good and bad, pain and pleasure, gain and loss. The simplest way to live is to cultivate equanimity in our hearts and join in the dance of opposites. Then we can navigate our way through depression and despair as well as delight and pleasure.

Elegant simplicity is a spiritual path as well as a practical way of life. It is the harbinger of harmony and sustainer of the social fabric. Elegant simplicity preserves natural habitats as well as protects cultures and communities. Elegant simplicity is as good for the outer landscape of the ecosphere as it is good for the inner landscape of the soul.

The way to sustainability is simplicity. No amount of technological innovation will be enough. We have to simplify our homes, our workplaces, and our lives. That is the way to create a sustainable world both now and forever.

Simplicity is also the way to spirituality. No number of temples, churches, mosques, or holy books will be of any help unless we think simply and free ourselves from the burdens of fear, anger, ego, and greed. With outer and inner simplicity, we can live a life of environmental stability, spiritual fulfillment, and social justice. Elegant simplicity is as much a world view as it is a lifestyle.

That is the content of this book.

— Satish Kumar
Hartland, Devon

my story:
beginnings

Human happiness
lies in contentment.
Mahatma Gandhi

In the deserts of Rajasthan in India, in a house by a plum tree, I was born on 9th August 1936. There was no electricity, and no radio, no TV, no telephone, no car, and no computers. But there were camels and cows, fields and farms, songs and stories, arts and crafts, dance and music aplenty. I grew up in the care of my kind mother. My father died when I was four years old. My grief-stricken mother found me a source of solace; that's what she said. Although I received a lot of love and longing from her, she could not hide her broken heart from me or anyone else.

My father died of a heart attack when he was 50 years old, and left my mother, ten years younger, to take care of me and my seven brothers and sisters. Though often in tears, she looked after us with enormous courage, and yet, as a small child, I could not help but witness her sorrow, her loss, and her loneliness.

As time passed, I began to notice a change. My mother started to practice meditation. I would hear her singing mantras about equanimity; acceptance of pain and pleasure, gain and loss; of birth and death as existential reality. While meditating, the dark shadow of sorrow lifted from her face and a strong atmosphere of resilience emanated from her whole body. These meditations led her into a deeper state of being. In place of tears in her eyes, I saw a gracious clarity glowing from them.

She would take me to our small farm, walking and talking about trees, bees, and butterflies. She would speak about the healing power of Nature and about Nature as our teacher. I remember those wonderful walks being full of fun and fascination. She would tell stories and sing songs.

I loved the way she walked and talked and laughed. I loved the way she could remember those wonderful long stories which gripped my attention. I always wanted to walk with my mother to our farm. I was happy to think that she was my mother, and that she knew and remembered so much. I was fortunate to have had such a mother; she was my mentor, my teacher, my guru, and my hero. She embodied elegant simplicity.

When I look back and reflect, I am amazed to remember her life being transformed from a state of loss and loneliness to a state of serenity, stability, and contentment. I remember her being a beautiful mother, a good gardener, and a happy homemaker. I remember her as a woman who had dropped her fears, someone who celebrated the present, every moment of it, and someone who trusted the future without doubts or desires. She was hardly ever angry.

My mother had become reconciled to the death of my father, but I grew sadder and sadder. As a boy of seven and eight, I could not forget the days when my mother had been gripped by grief. The days when she used to suddenly start sobbing, and I wondered, "Why did my father die? What is death? Will my mother die too? Will I die also?" Nobody could answer these questions to my satisfaction, not even my mother. "Yes, one day I too will die, you too will die, we will all die. We are caught in an unending cycle of birth and death." This was the answer my mother gave me. But these answers made me anxious and discontented.

I wanted someone to tell me, "Yes, there is something you can do to stop people dying. Yes, you can have a life without death." No one, but no one, uttered such words in my ears.

Then one day I spoke with a revered Jain monk called Tulsi. His name meant basil, sacred basil—so simple and so ordinary—but he was anything but ordinary. Tulsi was my mother's guru and the guru of our family. The guru of tens of thousands of followers, seeking salvation. People called him Gurudev, Guru divine. People adored him, worshipped him.

When I met him, he was only 30 years old. He was handsome and happy. People thought of him as an enlightened being. Like everyone else, I was mesmerized by him, he felt to me like the father I had lost. But he was more than that, he was the embodiment of serenity and peace. And above all, he spoke the words I'd longed to hear for so long: "Yes, you can bring an end to the cycle of birth and death, you can obtain nirvana, the ultimate liberation, freedom from worldly comings and goings. Yes, you can be free from loss, loneliness, and every other kind of suffering." These words came from the lips of a man who had discovered the truth and who was believed by everyone.

"What must I do to obtain nirvana?" I asked him.

"You have to renounce the world and follow the way of the monks. Let go of your pride and possessions. Free yourself from the bondage of family and attachment to wealth. You need to live the life of a monk," Gurudev answered in a firm and matter of fact manner.

"I want to be with you Gurudev! I will do anything to defeat death. I want to be a monk!" These words came out of my mouth without any thought or hesitation. My heart was throbbing. My body was shaking. My mind was overwhelmed with the prospect of walking alongside Gurudev Tulsi. I felt safe with him.

Many people thought I had an old soul in a new body. In India it is believed that we are reincarnated and carry our karma from previous lives. So my attraction to monks may have been something to do with the karma from previous lives.

I was fortunate that my mother—somewhat reluctantly—understood. She said to me, "If that is your calling and your destiny, then who am I to be an obstacle to your spiritual seeking?" Other family members and some of my mother's friends were not so open or generous. "How can a boy of nine know what is his calling or his destiny?" This was the argument my brothers made, and the answer my mother gave them was filled with emotion and conviction: "I know, I know. It is hard for me to let this little boy leave me, but a child is not an underdeveloped adult. If we dampen or discourage his desire to seek a spiritual life now, how do we know what will be the effect on his tender soul? It is not easy, but on balance, we have to let him do what he wants to do."

My brothers were amazed, but my mother's words gladdened my heart. She loved me but did not want to possess me. I believe it was she who laid the foundation of courage and activism in my life by being bold and selfless enough to let me leave home and follow the path of peace. Eventually, I even persuaded the most skeptical of my brothers to give his permission and allow me to become a wandering sadhu.

I left my home behind. I let go of the ties of love with my beloved mother. I held a begging bowl in my hand, taking food only once a day. I walked barefoot chanting the sacred mantra, "Om...Om...Om."

"Pay no attention to worldly affairs. Read no books other than the sacred scriptures of the Jains. Learn the holy texts by heart and meditate upon them day and night." Thus spoke my Gurudev. "Burn up all your lingering negativities from the past by the austere practices of asceticism."

So I took no bath for nine years. My thick black hair was plucked out by hand twice a year. I fasted for 24 hours, then 48 hours, then three days every month. I sat in silence for two hours in the morning and two hours in the evening focusing on *atman*, my intimate and eternal self, merging with *paramatman*, the ultimate and boundless spirit of pure light.

After listening to my guru and reading some of the Jain scriptures, I started to look at my body as bondage, the world as a trap, and my meditation was to free myself from pride and greed, from anger and ego, from desires and doubts, so that I would be cleansed of all sins.

This went on for years and years. It felt like a long time of longing for that elusive liberation, or *moksha*. I was entering my teenage years, I was 14, 15. I made my meditations last longer and my fasts more frequent. I went walking in solitude, searching salvation. Then I was 16 and 17. "I must try harder to find freedom in my soul," I said to myself. "What more can I do? Oh god of death, Kala, come to me, come soon and free me from this sinful body, free me from this weary world," I begged. I remember that period of despondency vividly. I wanted to die, and never return to this world.

Then a lay disciple, Kishor, having sensed my state of turmoil, dared to give me a book by Mahatma Gandhi. I was not allowed to read any nonreligious books, including Gandhi's, but I read this book in secret. It challenged my troubled mind. That night Gandhi came to me in a dream. He was walking up a hill, I was down below. Then he sat down. He waited for me. When I reached him, he said, "To find salvation you don't have to forsake the world." He stood up and said, "Come with me." He walked a few steps higher and continued, "Practice spirituality through serving the world, not renouncing the world. Renounce your passion, your lust, and your desires; and thus transform your life and find salvation." As Gandhi spoke these words, a light surrounded him and lifted him up until he disappeared into clouds, as if he had attained nirvana.

I woke up sweating. It must have been past midnight. I kept tossing and turning in confusion. What did Gandhi mean?

In the morning, I decided to go for a long walk to calm my mind. I walked out of the town of Ratangarh which was surrounded by sand dunes. I crossed one dune after another, going nowhere. I thought of my Gurudev; he was very dear to me. He had taught me much about the futility of worldly affairs and about the art of renunciation. Gurudev was gracious, benevolent, and learned. But he was teaching me to let go of something—the world—which I didn't know. Suddenly a deep desire grew in my heart. I wanted to embrace the world and love the world. I wanted to plant flowers. I wanted to grow and cook food instead of begging for it. I wanted to hold a beautiful woman in my arms and touch her lips with my lips. I wanted a home where I could live without moving on constantly, and sleep in a soft bed rather than on a hard floor.

Something had changed in me most profoundly. My fear of death had faded. My wish—my need—to end the cycle of birth and death seemed like a distant memory.

I had walked a long way. I had lost my sense of time. I remember walking for hours and hours and not knowing where I was. Certainly it was late afternoon, the sun was moving westwards. I was tired, hungry, and thirsty, and there was no one in sight. I had never been in this part of the desert before, I did not know my way back to the town. I was lost within and I was lost without. I was walking in circles, looking this way and that, trying to figure out which direction the town might be.

After a while, which felt like an eternity, I saw a man with a camel in the distance. With a sense of relief, I called out to him, and he stopped. He must have realized that I, in my white robe, must be a lost monk. We walked toward each other.

"I am lost," I said, "and I am very thirsty. Do you have any water?"

The kind camel man smiled at me and said, "You should never travel in the desert without water!" Then he passed me his clay water bottle, which was covered in a wet cloth to keep it cool. I drank and drank the water, then I said, "I nearly died of thirst in this desert. Water is life. Thank you camel man, thank you! Thank you for saving my life. What is your name?"

"People call me Krishna," he said.

"God Krishna himself, no less!" I laughed.

"My parents wanted me to be as joyful as Lord Krishna, so they named me thus," said the camel man. "Krishna was a keeper of cows, he was a happy farmer. So am I, I am happy."

I was touched by the manner of his speech, he spoke with ease and delight.

"Which way are you going?" I asked.

"I live in a small village near Ratangarh."

"Can I follow you? I have lost my way."

"Of course. Do you want a ride on my camel?"

"No, no, I am a monk, I have not ridden a camel nor a horse, nor a car nor a train, nor a boat, nor even a bicycle for nine years. I must walk. That is my rule."

I followed Krishna. He wore a red turban and had silver rings in his ears. His *kurta* (shirt) was orange and made of coarse cotton. The camel was loaded with farm produce: millet, melons, and sesame seeds. I remembered my childhood. My mother used to grow the same. I learned that Krishna never went to school, so he could not read or write. But he could look after camels and grow food for his family. He had built his own house with clay, wood, and straw. His wife milked cows, made butter and yogurt, sang folk songs, and looked after their two children. Krishna explained all this to me enthusiastically. He lived a simple but delightful life.

"Where did you learn all these skills? Would you not have liked to go to school?" I asked.

"I learned from my father and mother, but more than that I learned by doing. I am in the school of nature, nature is my teacher. I learn from the land all the time," Krishna replied. It was pure peasant wisdom. He sounded like my mother. Walking with Krishna for over an hour revived me.

"How do you learn from the land?" I probed.

"Just listening to the land and looking around. Look at these sand dunes, they always shift, move, and change, yet they always remain the same. Even in this dry desert, we get monsoon rains. Even in this barren-looking land, we grow millet and melons. I love this land. The sand shines under the moonlight like fields of silver. The land is beautiful and benign."

I could have listened to Krishna for hours.

We reached Ratangarh. Walking back calmed me, and at the same time, I yearned to be like Krishna, normal and ordinary. Krishna made me think, who am I? Am I defined by my white robe? Am I more than a monk? More than my name? More than my robe and my appearance? Suddenly I saw a clear light. I said to myself, I am free. I saw a bird flying out of the cage of my body.

And I was free.

That was it. My shoulders were light. The weight was off.

I went back to the house where I was spending the monsoon season with two other monks. They were very dear to me. I wanted to let them know my state of mind. We talked for hours. To my surprise and delight, they also wanted to be free of the constraints of the order. The three of us wanted to leave. A few days later, I managed to persuade a woman disciple to give us some ordinary clothes and train fares to Delhi, which she did.

That night, after midnight, when the town was asleep and the streets were dark, we ran away from the confines of the monastic order. I escaped the prison of my own choosing. I was filled with mixed emotions—rebellion and gratitude. Gurudev had given me so much love, so much training, so much of himself. But now I must find my own inner guru and not be dependent on Gurudev Tulsi for the rest of my life. I was no longer looking to conquer death, I was looking to embrace life with all its uncertainties, ambiguities, and struggles.

Of course, Gurudev was sad and felt betrayed. My mother was upset and angry. She rejected me and refused to have anything to do with me, let alone have me back at her home. (I write more about this in Chapter 10.) This proved to be a blessing in disguise. I remembered my dream of Gandhi and his words about spirituality in the world, in everyday life, in every thought, word, and action.

So I took refuge in an ashram, a community of people engaged in spiritual activism. The ashram was in the sacred city of Bodh Gaya, near the Bodhi tree under which Buddha had been enlightened. It was a perfect environment for me. My wish was not to escape spirituality. Simply, I felt I was moving away from the duality of the worldly versus the spiritual. This was my reunion with the world.

The ashram had been established by Vinoba Bhave, a close friend of Gandhi. He taught that the holy spirit permeates matter through and through and makes it holy. Matter and spirit cannot be separated. Spirituality is not a system of beliefs or a set of dogmas or doctrines. Spirituality is a way of life. Religions and rituals, holy books and temples, may help to open the doors of perception, but we have to go beyond them in order to experience a living spirituality, in the ordinary simplicity of everyday life. For this to occur, we need to live in harmony with ourselves, our fellow humans, and the natural world.

The words of Vinoba, communicated to me by the ashramites, were music to my ears. Here I was anonymous, no one needed to bow to me, and I had no need to pretend to be holy. I was liberated from my vanity. After nine years, I was touching the soil again. I worked in the garden and in the kitchen. It felt strange and good. I breathed the air of emancipation.

Paradoxically, monkhood had made me feel suffocated and resilient at the same time. By giving up my home, my school, my friends, and leaving my mother behind—and then, as a monk, handling no money for nine years, having no home, and no possessions—I had learned the art of renunciation. Yet I had never felt the lack of anything. I had been detached from desires. As a monk, I had learned that fear is the root cause of ego, anger, greed, and pride. So I must drop fear and trust the unknown. I was grateful for this gift from my guru. Now I was pleased to live without fear in the real world, and not be sheltered in the glass house of a monastic order. I had made the biggest U-turn of my life.

At the ashram, I learned about the four stages of life according to the Hindu tradition. The first 25 years is the period of learning, when the foundation for the rest of life is laid. The second 25 years is for practicing the skills and ideas you have acquired. The third period of 25 years is for committing yourself to the service of your community and society. And the fourth and final stage is for living your inner truth through meditation, reflection, renunciation, and letting go of all attachments to material and emotional possessions. This ideal pattern of life is one I cherish, and it has guided my actions.

As a monk, I learned the arts of walking, fasting, thinking, and meditating. At the ashram in Bodh Gaya, I learned the arts of making—cooking, gardening, and spinning cotton into yarn to make my own clothes. With Vinoba I learned how to meditate while making and how to be still while walking.

Vinoba Bhave was a peace pilgrim on a mission to bring about a kingdom of compassion. He walked over 100,000 miles, and everywhere he went, he asked landlords to share their land with the poor. I too became a peace pilgrim with a mission to end the nuclear arms race. I walked eight thousand miles to the countries possessing nuclear bombs. In those two and a half years, I realized that pilgrimage is as much a metaphor as it is a literal reality. To be a pilgrim is to live lightly and simply in all circumstances, to embrace both delights and difficulties with equanimity they present themselves. Although I have made many pilgrimages to holy places and sacred shrines of religious and natural significance, but the deeper truth is that life itself is a pilgrimage.

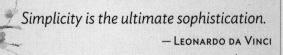

Simplicity is the ultimate sophistication.
— LEONARDO DA VINCI

simplicity of walking

All truly great thoughts
are conceived by walking.

Friedrich Nietzsche

My nine years as a Jain monk were a time of training in peace. Jains have made the meaning of peace as wide and as deep as possible, Jains were, and to a large extent still are, the original and staunchest pacifists of India; they have always advocated the practice of peace in such a manner that, from time to time, they have been labeled practitioners of extreme nonviolence—they will not even kill a mosquito, never mind killing an animal or a human! Jains are allowed to ordain monks and nuns at an early age. I became so deeply and profoundly attracted to our Jain guru, Acharya Tulsi, that I persuaded my mother to let me leave home to follow the way of the Jains and live and learn the principles of peace when I was only nine years old.

I remained a Jain monk for nine years. It was a time of training in peace. The most important training of all was walking barefoot. For nine years, I rode no animals, traveled in no cars or trains, no boats, bicycles, or airplanes. Yet I walked thousands of miles—through deserts and jungles, across mountains and plains, in hot and cold conditions. I had no home and no money, no storage, no possessions. I begged for food once a day and ate what I was given, keeping no leftovers overnight. I possessed only what I could carry on my body. Walking was not just a means of traveling from A to B, not just a means of arriving somewhere. Walking was a spiritual practice in itself—a practice in simplicity, minimalism, and meditation.

Monkhood, then, was my preparation for the realization of peace within. "How can you make peace in the world if you are not at peace within yourself?" my guru asked. "Peace is not only what you think or what you say but how you are. Making peace begins with being peace; there is no distinction between the liquidity of milk, the whiteness of milk, and the nutritious qualities of milk. The consistency, color, and quality of milk are an integrated whole; similarly, thinking, speaking, and being peace must be integrated. Then peace will radiate from you as effortlessly as light radiates from the sun."

When, at the age of 18, I left the life of a mendicant and joined a peace activist, a follower of Mahatma Gandhi called Vinoba Bhave, I added the social dimension of peace to the spiritual dimension I had acquired as a young Jain monk. "There can be no peace in the world while the powerful dominate the dispossessed and the rich exploit the poor," Vinoba explained. "India is now free from the British Raj and colonial rule, but India is still not free. As long as landlords live in luxury and landless laborers toil for starvation wages, there can be no peace even if there is an appearance of calm."

Armed with this conviction, Vinoba went from landlord to landlord, asking them not to wait for an armed uprising or government legislation, but to act out of the compassion of their hearts and in response to a political call for social justice. He said they should act right away to make peace with their neighbors and peace with their peasants by sharing their land with them. This was the Land Gift movement to establish political peace.

I was so deeply inspired when I met Vinoba that I decided, as I had no land to give to the cause, to give instead the gift of my life. Vinoba, like me, walked. Jeeps and cars cannot reach where your legs can reach—not only the remote villages and hamlets, but also the hearts of the people. I was ready for that. I had already walked thousands of miles, so my feet were toughened, my muscles were hardened, and my resolve was resilient.

"What should I say to the landlords to persuade them to give up their most precious possession—their land?" I asked Vinoba.

"Tell them, if you have five children, consider Vinoba your sixth child, representing the poor, the wretched, and the weak. Give one sixth of your land. If one sixth of the land of India was redistributed among the landless farm laborers, then no one would be left without a source of livelihood."

"But this seems too idealistic, Vinoba," I protested. "People are bound to resist, thinking, 'We own this land, we inherited it from our parents, it is our land, why should we give it away?'"

Vinoba replied, "How can anyone own the land? It belongs to Nature. Do you own the air? Does anyone own water? Does sunshine belong to anyone? We cannot claim ownership of Nature and the basic elements of life, we can only live in relationship with them."

Vinoba continued, "In any case, if we do not share the land, then the poor and dispossessed are not going to take it lying down forever. Do we want a violent revolution? Is it not better to bring about change in a sensible, rational, and peaceful manner?"

Equipped with such sincere, uplifting, and convincing thoughts, I went with fellow peace activists and campaigners to a landlord who was at the same time the head of a Hindu Temple owning two thousand acres of prime paddy fields.

But how would we get to see him?

"Please tell the High Priest that some messengers from Vinoba wish to see him." I told the staff at the Temple office.

The staff frowned but offered us a glass of water. They knew that Vinoba was no ordinary person; he was, apart from being a radical land reformer and peacemaker, also a renowned Hindu scholar whose talks on the Gita, one of the sacred texts of India, had sold millions of copies in more than a dozen languages. And yet we were refused an audience with the Temple's High Priest.

It was not that he did not have time to see us, rather that he did not wish to entertain the idea of parting with some land in favor of the landless. And so even before we had the chance to present our vision, the values and the ideals of land reform through peaceful means, we had been rejected outright.

What then should we do?

The following day, we prepared some banners and a dozen of us returned to the Temple office very early in the morning and before the High Priest arrived. Our banner had no radical slogans. The only demand we printed on it was: We wish to meet the High Priest.

As we saw the jeep that he traveled in approaching the Temple, we moved to block the gate. And because the jeep had no doors, there was no physical barrier between us and the High Priest. We surrounded the vehicle so it could not move forward or backward.

"What do you want?" the High Priest asked.

"We want an audience with you."

"But I am very busy," he replied.

"But the poor are very hungry," we said.

"I will arrange to provide food for them. Now, let me go."

"But they will be hungry again tomorrow, and the day after, and the day after that. How long can you go on feeding them? We want to do something that will enable them to feed themselves."

The High Priest fell silent.

"I know what you want. You want me to give land," he said.

"Yes, that's right. Then the poor and the hungry can feed themselves forever and without disturbing or bothering you. You will gain peace of mind, and you will be living in a happy neighborhood. For yourself, you will gain merit and a good reputation. People will sing your praises. When you are kind to the poor and generous to those who have nothing, you yourself will be happy."

This is how we pleaded with him.

"I have to consult with my committee. And in any case, why don't you yourselves raise some funds to buy the land? I would certainly contribute toward such a fund. I am sure we could give a thousand rupees. Even five thousand rupees. That would be a much better way. I just don't think we can give you land," the High Priest told us.

We were delighted that we were having such a dialogue with him at the gate to the office near the Temple. People from the street started to gather around to listen, and the Temple officials were looking worried.

"Please clear the way, the High Priest must attend to his

appointments," said one of those officials, But we paid no heed to his request.

I said to the High Priest, "There are millions of people in our country who have no home, no land and no livelihood. How much money can we raise to buy the land for these teeming millions? This is why Vinoba, in pursuing a spiritual solution, is advocating Land Gift. He says money is the problem, not the solution. Gift is the solution. The giving of a gift is as beneficial to the giver as it is to the receiver."

"Let me think about it," the High Priest replied.

"Can we come and see you tomorrow morning? That will give you 24 hours to think," I replied. "We are not asking for anything ourselves. Vinoba has no home, he lives in an ashram and walks around the country collecting land for the poor. So please remember, giving the land to Vinoba for the poor is as much in your interest as it is in the interest of the recipients—the landless laborers and farm workers. Please also remember Vinoba's message that the land does not belong to us, we belong to the land. When we die, we do not take it with us. This is why Vinoba is asking us to share and care—so that you and your workers are happy together."

I had found myself in a strange position, reminding the High Priest of a Hindu Temple of the highest of Hindu ideals.

He smiled at me and said, "All right, come and see me tomorrow morning. We will see what we can do."

We clapped. Everybody clapped. Yesterday, we had wanted a private audience with the High Priest. Today, we had been given a very public audience, which had proved much better for us.

The next morning, the staff at the Temple office were much more cooperative. As soon as we arrived, we were given glasses of water and cups of tea, and very soon we were ushered into the presence of the High Priest. Before we could utter a single word, the High Priest told us, "I know Vinoba is a great spirit, he is a man of compassion and commitment to the uplifting of the poor, so please take this note from us to Vinoba."

The note said: "We wish to donate 120 acres of our land to Vinoba for redistribution among the landless farm workers. Please arrange for your colleagues to work with our staff to locate the area of land precisely and mark it out."

It was an easy success for us, and we were over the moon.

This was happening all over India. Between 1951 and 1971, four million acres of land were donated to Vinoba in a similar manner. This was social activism at its best. And during those years, Vinoba himself walked over a hundred thousand miles covering the length and breadth of India, from Kashmir to Kerala, from Goa to Assam. I had the great good fortune of walking with him and working with him as an apprentice activist.

One morning in 1961, my friend E. P. Menon and I went to a café for our morning coffee and breakfast. E. P. was born in Kerala, South India. He and I worked closely together in the Gandhian movement and walked with Vinoba Bhave. He was a keen campaigner for political change and also a keen reader of literature such as the novels of Tolstoy. At this time, we had both been assigned by Vinoba to work at an ashram near Bangalore, a city of culture and commerce with a cool climate and famous cafés and restaurants. We were deeply grateful to Vinoba for giving us the opportunity to establish an ashram where young activists like ourselves could be trained and inspired.

On this particular day, we were to encounter a piece of news that would change the course of both of our lives forever. While we waited for our coffee, we read in the newspaper that a 90-year-old philosopher and Nobel Prize-winning mathematician had been sentenced to a week in jail for protesting against nuclear weapons in Britain. Reading such an extraordinary story, we were surprised, amazed, and shocked. Although I was already deeply committed to the idea of nonviolence and world peace, I was astonished to learn of a Western philosopher of great age who followed the Gandhian way and was going to jail with the courage of his conviction.

The man was, of course, the British peace activist, Bertrand Russell. We felt challenged to do something to support this philosopher, who had shown such enormous courage and conviction—but what? We then learned that Bertrand Russell and thousands of other protesters against nuclear weapons were marching from Aldermaston to London. Out of the blue, a thought came to us: why don't we walk from Delhi to Moscow, Paris, London, and Washington—the capital cities of all those countries in possession of nuclear weapons at the time.

"Wow!" We'd found our inspiring idea. We were going to walk to all four nuclear capitals of the world.

We flew to Assam, where Vinoba was walking for Land Gift. It was not hard to find him. Both the newspaper and the radio covered his every move, and anyone who was anyone knew where he was. He was not only the talk of the town but the talk of the state of Assam!

We reached Vinoba in a remote village where he had just arrived after walking for ten miles. When he saw us he said, "What brings you so unexpectedly? Are you okay? How is everything and everyone in Bangalore?"

We were apprehensive. After giving news of the ashram, we revealed that we had come specifically to ask for his permission, support, and blessing to undertake a mission for world peace and the cessation of nuclear weapons.

Vinoba was a true saint—selfless, detached, and unperturbed. "Interesting." he said. "Will you walk all the way? Which route will you take?" He asked us to show him a map of the countries through which we would walk. We had a long conversation about the route and the advantages and disadvantages of various alternatives. Then suddenly he pushed the map aside.

"Yes, you have my blessing, but I give you two weapons to protect you on this long journey. Firstly, you are vegetarians and must remain so, and secondly, you must walk without a penny in your pockets."

We were stunned.

"Remaining vegetarian we understand, Vinoba, but when you say take no money, do you really mean that we must have no money at all? What if we need to buy a cup of tea or make a telephone call?"

Vinoba told us, "Either you should have a lot of money, like a king, or you should have no money and so live like a sadhu." He laughed and continued, "War begins in fear of others, and peace emerges out of trust. It is no good just preaching peace; to be a true peacemaker, you have to practice peace, which means practicing trust. So, you go on this great journey with trust in your hearts. Trust people and trust the process of the universe and all shall be well."

But we were still apprehensive and unsure. "Surely we trust people, but for convenience sake, could we not just carry a little money with us?"

Vinoba gave us the practical reason for walking with no money at all. "When you arrive in a place after a long walk, you will feel tired and exhausted. If you have money, you will eat in a restaurant, sleep in a guest house, and walk away the next day. But when you have no money, you will be forced to find someone who can give you hospitality for the night. They will offer you food, and you will say you are vegetarians and they will ask why? And then your communication about peace can begin."

Vinoba was my guru, and the relationship between a novice and a guru is of complete and unquestioning surrender to the guru's guidance and wisdom. In any case, having lived without money for nine years as a Jain monk, I was marginally more prepared than Menon. But even then he was courageous enough to say, "Yes, let our journey be a pilgrimage."

Having received Vinoba's blessings, we went to New Delhi, to Raj Ghat, to the grave of Mahatma Gandhi and began our pilgrimage, not only without money but even without passports. The Indian government in those days required us to place a deposit of twenty thousand rupees. In case we had to be repatriated for any reason, the deposit would be there to cover those costs. This was a good test for us—whether or not to trust the Indian government would grant us passports. The Indian newspapers covered the story of our pilgrimage, and a member of parliament raised the question with the Prime Minister, Mr. Nehru himself. "Why are peace pilgrims denied their birthright of free citizenship, unrestricted travel, and a passport?"

Mr. Nehru at that time was not only the Prime Minister but also Minister for Foreign Affairs. We had already informed him of our plans, and we had received an encouraging response and his good wishes. So he took personal responsibility to cut through the bureaucratic red tape, and on the day before we were scheduled to cross the border into Pakistan, two officials arrived in search of us and delivered our passports. Trust had prevailed.

Then, equipped with our passports, we were standing at the border of India and Pakistan ready to depart. Thirty-five men and women came to bid us farewell. Most were enthusiastic about our plans, but one woman friend of ours was rather worried and concerned.

"Aren't you crazy, my friends, to walk into Pakistan? We are at war with that country, they are our enemies. You have no money, no food, and you are on foot. What about your safety and security?" She spoke to us scoldingly. "Forget Vinoba, at least you should carry some food with you, here are some packets of food to sustain you while you are looking around for a sympathetic host."

This was a moment of trial. I thought for a minute, reflecting on Vinoba's words, and said to my friend, "Thank you for your kindness, but these packets of food are not packets of food, they are packets of mistrust. What are we going to say to our Pakistani hosts? We didn't know whether you would feed us or not so we have brought our own food all the way from India. So please understand and forgive us for refusing your kind offer." The woman was in tears.

"Why are you crying my friend? Please give us your blessing."

"Satish, this might be my last chance of seeing you. You are going to Muslim countries, capitalist countries, deserts, jungles, mountains, snowstorms, and you have no food and no money to support you. I cannot imagine that you will survive this ordeal and return alive." My friend was really sobbing now.

"Don't worry, my dear friend, if I die while walking for peace, that is the best kind of death I can have. So from today, I will walk for peace without fearing death and without fearing hunger. If I don't get food some days, I will consider it my opportunity to fast, and if I don't get shelter some days, I will take it as an opportunity to sleep in a hotel of a million stars. Surely that will be better than a five-star hotel!"

But even that joke did not satisfy my friend. She hugged me tight, still sobbing, but she also realized that there was no way to stop me. Whether we faced life or death, Menon and I were determined to go.

To our great surprise, as soon as we stepped onto the soil of Pakistan, a young man approached us and enthusiastically asked, "Are you the two walkers coming to Pakistan for peace?"

"Yes we are, but how did you know? We don't know anyone in Pakistan. We've written to nobody in your country, and yet you seem to know all about us. How come?"

"Your fame has traveled ahead of you. I read about you in the local papers, and some other travelers, also coming from India, had seen you and talked about you. When I heard that there were two Indians putting out their hands in friendship, I was touched and moved. I have been looking for you for days. I am also for peace. What nonsense that India and Pakistan should be at war."

The stranger continued, "Before 1947, we were one people. We cannot choose anything other than to be neighbors and friends, and so I have come to welcome you."

His words were music to our ears. I told him, "Thank you, you have a big heart and a big mind. Peace cannot be achieved through mean-mindedness. If we come here as Indians, we meet Pakistanis. If we come here as Hindus, we meet Muslims. But if we come as human beings, then we meet human beings."

I carried on explaining, "Being a Hindu, a Muslim, or an Indian or Pakistani, these are our secondary identities. Being members of the human community and the Earth community is our primary identity."

The young man, Gulam Yasin, gave us both a hearty hug and offered the hospitality of his home. Five minutes earlier, my friend had been sobbing, filled with fear of Muslim Pakistani enemies, and here we were, just moments later, embracing one! This was repeated day after day and night after night across Pakistan. Again and again, people proclaimed that war is not between Hindus and Muslims or between Indians and Pakistanis—war is between power-seeking politicians and profit-seeking manufacturers of the weapons of war.

Whether we were walking on the plains of Pakistan or the heights of the Khyber pass, whether we were being entertained by the Rotarians of Rawalpindi or by the spirited Pathans of Pakistan, the cry of ordinary people in the street was the same—don't waste our wealth or talent on weapons of hatred, do something to enhance the harmony and well-being of those who work in the fields, the factories, the schools, and the hospitals.

Blisters aside, we were blessed by the generosity of human hearts throughout our journey, crossing the hills of Afghanistan, the sandstorms of Iran, and the lush vineyards of Azerbaijan. Having no money proved to be a blessing rather than an impediment. The moment people realized that we were pilgrims of peace who had renounced dependence on money, they were more eager than ever to help us and much more eager than if we had carried money.

The cool stillness of the Caspian Sea, the imposing grandeur of Mount Ararat, the sumptuous orchards of Armenia, the deep green tea gardens of Georgia were as inspiring as the people of these countries. I have written about the transformative experience of the kindness we received during our journey in my book *No Destination*, but I would like to retell the story of the "peace tea" which gave our pilgrimage a particular focus.

Black Sea on the left, Caucasus Mountains on our right, we trudged along day after day. "Are we really achieving anything?" I asked my companion Menon, with no little desperation in my despondent voice.

"Are you feeling low?" he asked. "Remember it is all about action and not about results. Come on, pull yourself together."

As Menon was speaking, I was reminded of the famous song of Rabindranath Tagore:

If no one comes to your call,
Even then, walk alone, walk alone.
Even if everyone looks away

Speak alone, speak alone.
Even when the path gets tough
Tramp alone, tramp alone…

Tagore's words helped me somewhat, but not enough. I was still overcome with doubt. However, just then I noticed two young women standing enjoying the sunshine. I gave them a leaflet, written in Russian, which described the purpose, the route, and our action for peace. One of them said, "We heard you on the radio, what a coincidence that we should meet you. Have you really walked all the way from India?"

"Yes we have!"

"Our Saint Rasputin went to India on foot. Are you making a return journey?"

"You could say so," we replied, in the basic Russian that we had been learning. We were about to walk away when one of the women said, "We work in a tea factory, it is our lunch break, would you like a cup of tea in our canteen and tell us all about your journey?"

"Of course," we replied. "Anytime is tea time!"

We followed the women back to the factory, dropped our rucksacks to the ground, and started to relax over a cup of tea. Some of the Soviet workers started to gather around us; seeing strangers from India was very novel to them. Soon biscuits and bread also arrived, and Menon and I were delighted to sit down, enjoy the delicious cup of tea, and answer question after question. The curiosity of these workers was boundless. This may have been a remote rural location, but their concern for peace and their amazement at the stupidity of the militarists wasting resources on useless nuclear weapons filled the room. While we were deeply engaged in a discussion about disarmament, one of the two women we had met originally had a brainwave. She suddenly stood up, went out of the room, and returned a moment later with four small packets of tea.

"I have a special request," she said. "These four packets of tea are for the four leaders of the nuclear countries of the world. I cannot reach these leaders, but I want you two to be our ambassadors and please be the messenger of this "peace tea" and deliver one packet to our Premier in the Kremlin, the second packet to the President of France in the Élysée Palace, the third packet to the Prime Minister of the UK, and the fourth packet to the President of the United States."

We listened to her request in complete silence. What an imaginative present!

"And please deliver the tea with a message from us, from this little factory by the Black Sea. Our message to them is this: This is no ordinary tea, this is peace tea, and if you ever get the mad thought of pressing the nuclear button, please hold for a moment and have a fresh cup of peace tea. This will give you a moment to reflect that your nuclear weapons will not only kill your enemies, they will kill all men, women, children, forests, birds, and lakes, in short, all of life. So think again and don't press the button."

"Wow!" I said "What a message."

I told Menon that all my despondency had disappeared. Come hell or high water, we would deliver these packets of peace tea to the desired destinations, just as the woman had requested. We thanked her for giving us such a special assignment. "We are honored to be your ambassadors of peace," we told her. The woman's face lit up. She was full of charm and grace and beauty. As she hugged us, everybody in the room clapped. This was the best sendoff we had ever had.

After many ups and downs, struggles and strife, we finally arrived in Moscow. Premier Nikita Khrushchev sent us a warm letter congratulating us but regretting that he could not meet us personally. However, we were invited to the Kremlin to deliver the packet of peace tea to the Chairman of the Supreme Soviet, Mr. Spiridonov, who would pass the gift to the Premier.

The splendor of the Kremlin was impressive, but what Mr. Spiridonov said on receiving the tea was less convincing. "Our Premier Khrushchev and the government are making proposal after proposal to the Western powers to safeguard peace. So your work is really there, in Western Europe and America, and I am glad that you are taking your message to them." Thus he had passed the buck!

From Moscow, through deep snow, we walked. Through Russian towns and villages as well as Belarusian, Polish, German, and Belgian rural and urban landscapes, we walked. It had taken us ten months to get to Moscow, and it took another six months to get to Paris. We were eager to see President De Gaulle, but all our letters and telephone calls had brought no response. So, with the support of French peace workers, Menon and I went to the Elysée Palace seeking an audience with the president or his representatives. But the guards, the officials, and the police all pressed us to move on as it was illegal to demonstrate or even assemble at the gates of the palace. As we refused to obey their orders, we were arrested and taken to prison, where we were threatened with deportation back to India. Eventually, after three days of negotiations that involved the

Indian Ambassador, we were allowed to deliver the peace tea to the head of the Paris police, who promised to pass it on to the palace. In a way, we were pleased to have been imprisoned in Paris since this really was our peace action—to follow in the footsteps of Bertrand Russell.

Helped by our French friends, we crossed the channel by boat and then walked from Dover to London, seeking a meeting with Prime Minister Harold Wilson. Again, the prime minister was too busy to meet with us; however, he asked Lord Atlee, the former prime minister, to receive us, and an official from the foreign ministry to meet us and accept the packet of peace tea on behalf of Mr. Wilson. On receiving us at the House of Lords, Lord Atlee said, "Dear chaps, be assured that no one is going to use nuclear weapons, it is only a show." He laughed, but the words of this short, slim, serene politician did not convince us.

"If that is the case, then why are we wasting our time and resources on these toys while people in the world starve, schools and hospitals lack resources, and children grow up in fear?"

"It's politics, youngsters, it's politics!" he replied. It was all very well for a retired politician to be so complacent, but he did promise that the packet of peace tea would have a place in 10 Downing Street, the home of the prime minister.

We met Bertrand Russell. That was a moment of exhilaration and inspiration. After our long chat and stories of our adventures, Lord Russell served us tea and cake, saying, "Make tea, not war!"

We crossed the Atlantic aboard the *Queen Mary* liner, thanks to financial support from various peace groups in the UK, and arrived in New York. We walked from there to Washington, D.C. President Johnson appointed his special assistant, Mr. Brooks Hays, to receive us in the White House, where he gave us a cordial welcome. In comparison with the Kremlin, the White House felt new and was far less spectacular, but the politics of the two places were not dissimilar.

"America leads the negotiations for peace at all international forums," Brooks Hays said. "It's the Soviets who create obstacles. As you have been there, I'm sure you know what they are like. Communism and peace are a contradiction in terms…what can we do?"

If President Johnson had a special assistant with such a closed mind, what hope was there for peace, I wondered. Nevertheless, we were given an undertaking that the packet of peace tea would be cherished by the President.

We did our best to be the ambassadors of the tea workers by the Black Sea, and that potent peace tea is still working. No nuclear weapons have been used, and fingers crossed, they never will be. However, these bombs are still there, and as long as they exist, I will continue to act for disarmament. That is my promise of peace activism.

Having walked eight thousand miles across 15 countries, I realized that peace is a state of mind and a way of life. I started with a search for inner peace as a Jain monk, then pursued political peace with the Land Gift movement, and followed that with a search for world peace by challenging the nuclear powers to declare unilateral disarmament. During this time, I became aware that I am held by the Earth, nourished by Nature, and sustained by rivers, forests, flowers, and wilderness. Unless we make peace with the planet, inner peace and world peace will remain elusive.

By walking across the continents and experiencing the workings of our modern civilization, I came to the conclusion that humanity is at war with Nature. During my walk, I witnessed the ways of industrial farming in Europe and in America, the way we extract and use natural resources, cutting down forests, overfishing the oceans, poisoning the land with chemicals, pesticides, and herbicides and emitting greenhouse gasses into the atmosphere—changing the very climate that sustains our lives. All these are acts of aggression against the Earth. Therefore, I became not only a peace activist but also an eco-activist, not only a peace pilgrim but an Earth pilgrim, and this way my activism is inclusive of inner peace, world peace, and green peace!

A fundamental fact is that in a finite planet we cannot afford to have an infinite amount of consumption, pollution, and waste. Therefore, living simply is a peace imperative. Even if there were no shortage of resources, ceaseless economic growth creates the burden of unnecessary clutter and unwanted stuff. People call it their high standard of living and go to war to protect these standards. However, in reality this is a war economy and a serious obstacle to a happy, comfortable, peaceful, and free life. Therefore, living simply is also a spiritual imperative.

> *In character, in manner of style, in all things, the supreme excellence is simplicity.*
> — HENRY WORDSWORTH LONGFELLOW

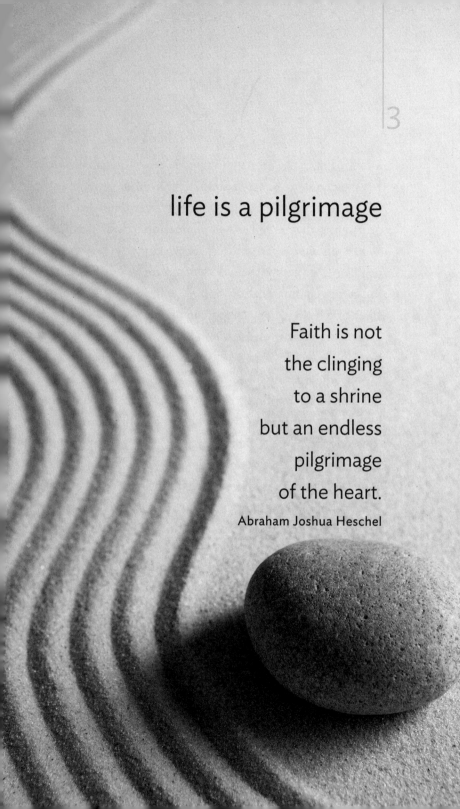

life is a pilgrimage

Faith is not
the clinging
to a shrine
but an endless
pilgrimage
of the heart.

Abraham Joshua Heschel

WHEN I MADE A PILGRIMAGE to Mount Kailash in Tibet, I walked on stony, steep, and hilly ground. I went up to 18,500 feet, crossing over a slippery glacier. The idea of pilgrimage is that very little is planned, fixed, or predicted. When difficulties arise, they are welcome. When we face problems, we accept them. Problems are an opportunity to use creativity, imagination, and ingenuity. They test our resilience. They challenge us to trust the universe.

If everything is planned and organized, if the hotels are prebooked, guides and taxis arranged, then we have no use for our imagination or ingenuity. These qualities are locked in a box. For example, if we have a suitcase full of nice clothes but no occasion to wear them, then what is the use of having those clothes? In the same way, if we have no opportunity to use our resilience and trust, then we are missing out on something important. Faced with difficulties, a pilgrim asks, "How shall I handle this problem? The universe has sent me a riddle, let me solve it calmly. Problems are welcome, stony ground is welcome." Pilgrims do not want a smooth tarmacked road, especially when walking. And pilgrimage is always better on foot.

The usual idea of pilgrimage is a journey to a sacred shrine or holy place. I have made such pilgrimages myself. But I have come to realize that the true meaning of pilgrimage is to live free from any attachments, habits, prejudices. Free from physical and mental clutter. Making an outer journey is a reminder of an inner journey, and I discovered that I am always on a pilgrimage. Life is a journey. I want to travel through life as a pilgrim.

Two people who fulfill my ideal of a pilgrim are Mahavir, the founder of Jainism, and Mahatma Gandhi, the father of India. They lived lives of simplicity par excellence. Neither of them feared difficulties. They believed that difficulties and sufferings are a means of purification. There is a famous legend about Mahavir which illustrates this. Mahavir was born a prince and became a monk. He renounced all material possessions. His followers always wanted him to come to their homes; they saw it as a privilege to give him food. Since begging was so easy, Mahavir wondered, "How do I make it difficult for myself to get food?" He believed that fear of difficulties can be overcome only by going through and experiencing them.

So he undertook an experiment, and according to legend he made the following vow: "I will take food only if it is given to me by a princess whose father has been defeated in battle. This princess should have been sold in the market place as a slave. And when this princess offers me food, she must offer me boiled lentils, nothing else. Furthermore, her foot should be chained, and there should be tears in her eyes. When these conditions are met, only then will I take food."

Can you imagine a test like this? So much stony ground to cross? He did not want the stones to be cleared from his path; he wanted stones put on the path to make his life difficult. So he went from house to house, from village to village, from town to town, looking for such a princess. Weeks passed. He was walking hungry. It so happened that there had been a battle between two kings in the territory where Mahavir was begging. One king was defeated. The victorious soldiers invaded the palace, took jewellery, weapons, clothes, and the princess. They said, "We will sell this princess and make lots of money." So they brought her to the marketplace and sold her as a slave. She was bought by a merchant. One day he had to go away on business and didn't want the princess to escape, so he shackled her ankle and chained her to the doorframe of the house. He said, "If you get hungry, here are some boiled lentils. Tomorrow I will return."

Mahavir came to this village, and eventually he passed by the merchant's house. He recognized the princess in chains, and she recognized him as Mahavir. She said, "In my misfortunes, at least you, Mahavir, great saint, have come to me. I am blessed! I have some boiled lentils to offer you." The princess was so happy. Mahavir looked at her. She was a princess, with a father defeated in a battle, she had been sold in the market place, and was chained by one foot with only boiled lentils to offer. All the conditions were met but one, she was smiling.

"I cannot take this food," Mahavir thought.

As he turned away, tears started to fall from the eyes of the princess. She cried out, "Even you, Mahavir, have abandoned me in my misfortune. I thought at least you would be kind and bless me by receiving some food from my hands."

Mahavir turned back and saw her tears. All his conditions were met. He cupped his hands before the princess, and she ladled lentils into them. At that moment, the heavens opened. Angels dropped rose petals from the sky in celebration, and the chain on the leg of the princess was released. The princess, Chandanbala, and Mahavir became enlightened, and together they founded the Jain religion.

This story is allegorical. It is not to be taken literally. The meaning of this legend is that the path of a pilgrim is not easy or straightforward. It involves struggle. We, in our modern world, are comfort seekers. We want everything to be made easy and convenient. We don't want to face difficulties or encounter problems. This makes us timid. We lack a sense of adventure, courage, confidence, and trust. We are reluctant to take risks. We lack faith in our ability to find our way over stony ground. We forget that before gold is made into jewellery it must go through fire.

Mahatma Gandhi was another champion of the simple life. He embodied the true spirit of a pilgrim. He endured imprisonment many times to achieve freedom for his people. In 1930 Gandhi protested against the British law to tax salt. He said, "This is a tax on the poor. I will boycott the law, and we will make salt without paying tax." He made a pilgrimage to the sea on foot from his ashram in Gujurat, and when he made salt, he was arrested and brought to court. The judge asked, "Mr. Gandhi, do you realize that you have broken the law and have incited other people to do the same? You must be punished." Gandhi said, "My Lord, I am a lawyer. I know I have broken the law. I plead guilty. Please give me the harshest punishment in the book. I have broken your unjust and immoral law. I want this law to be changed." The judge said, "All right, Mr. Gandhi, I have to send you to jail. But I hope that His Majesty's government will release you soon." Gandhi replied "My Lord, I will go to prison like a bridegroom goes to a wedding chamber. The point is not to release me from prison, the point is to change the law."

Gandhi was a pilgrim activist. He was on a sacred path. He struggled not for praise, or fame, or the Nobel Prize. He had no desire for any material gain or personal achievement. Gandhi followed the teachings of the Bhagavad Gita: "One should act without desiring the fruit of the action." In this way, he was true to the ideals of a pilgrim, whose action should be free of ego.

The act of pilgrimage has its own intrinsic value. A pilgrim is one who acts in the service of planet Earth and for self-realization and not to impress others. All difficulties, problems, and discomforts are part of their pilgrimage. They know in their heart that even the moments of great pleasure are temporary and will pass. Shakespeare expressed a profound wisdom when he said, "Rough winds do shake the darling buds of May."

It is time to live on this Earth as pilgrims and not as tourists. Pilgrims accept the gift of life and the gifts of Nature as they are given. Every moment is a moment of celebration; there is nothing to complain about. Pilgrims follow the advice, "I can't change the direction of the wind, but I can adjust my sails to reach my destination."

Pilgrims appreciate the sun, rain, flowers and fruit, as well as storms, wind, and blizzard. They accept life completely. Rabindranath Tagore expressed the ideal of a pilgrim when he said, "Clouds come floating into my life, no longer to carry rain or usher storm but to add color to my sunset sky." Pilgrims are free from the burden of expectations; when there are no expectations, there are no disappointments. They celebrate the present moment and trust that the universe has a bigger plan, and therefore they trust the process of the universe. "All shall be well and all manner of thing shall be well," as Saint Julian of Norwich said.

Going on a pilgrimage to a sacred site is a symbolic act to help us realize that life is always on the move. To go toward a sacred destination is ultimately to realize that the sacred place is within us. The outer and inner are one, staying and going are one. By making an outer journey, we make an inner journey.

Equipped with the spirit of celebration and trust, pilgrims participate in the process of life, participate in transformation, just as Mahavir and Mahatma Gandhi did. Thus a pilgrim's life is not one of passivity, rather it is a life of selfless action and selfless service.

For me elegant simplicity is rooted in the idea of pilgrimage. To be a pilgrim is to cultivate both outer simplicity and inner simplicity. Inner simplicity provides a profound base for outer simplicity.

Now let us explore the connection between simplicity and spirituality.

Simple can be harder than complex.
You have to work hard to make it simple.
But it's worth it in the end
because once you get there,
you can move mountains.

— STEVE JOBS

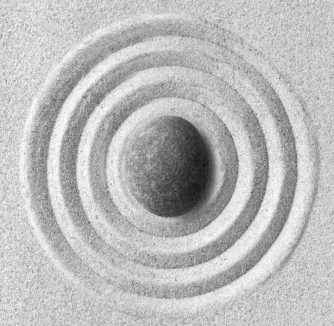

elegant simplicity

Any fool can
make things
complicated,
it requires a genius
to make them simple.

E. F. Schumacher

SIMPLICITY IS A MINDFUL WAY OF LIVING. At the mental level, at the level of feelings and relationships, at the level of home, clothes, and food—at every level—we must ask, how can I make life simple?

At the moment, in business, politics, and economics, we have made our lives very complicated. This puts so much burden on our shoulders, it makes us full of anxiety and worry. Therefore it is imperative to ask, how can I make my life simple? Just by asking this question every day, we may find an answer that leads to simplicity. Complicated ideas and thoughts going round and round in our heads create confusion. We need to calm down and ask: Do I have to go through all this or can I go straight to the heart of the matter? When we are talking with somebody, can we go straight to the point? Can we be clear and simple? Thus simplicity of mind, speech, and action is a continuum. A simple life is a spiritual life.

Material simplicity does not mean poverty. Living simply and without clutter does not mean that we should not have a comfortable life. There is an innate elegance in minimizing possessions and maximizing comfort. Clutter brings chaos, simplicity brings clarity. Simplicity is the voluntary acceptance of limits. In Japan there is a beautiful concept of *wabi sabi*. It means unpretentious, unselfconscious, and modest. Things need not be slick, glamorous, showy, or extravagant. They can be rough and ready. They can be natural and minimal. *Wabi sabi* is a way of practicing elegant simplicity. As Paulo Coelho said, "Elegance is achieved when all that is superfluous has been discarded."

To be minimal is beautiful. When we are speaking, it is better to use few words. Japanese haiku are very short. Great poetry does not need too many words. Simple and minimal, elegant, eloquent, and meaningful words make good poetry. In Sanskrit profound thoughts are expressed in short sutras and even shorter mantras. Sometimes even one word, like "Om," is enough.

In India we have the ideal of *satvik* which means authentic, simple, and truthful. *Satvik* food is natural and comes directly from a garden or straight from the fields, without so much packaging. Packaging makes things complicated. A supermarket is very complicated. We may go for one or two things and end up buying ten things. But if we go to a simple shop or a farmers' market where there is no plastic, no labels, no logos, no advertising, where things are simple and *satvik*, then we bring home the food that we need, and we prepare it with love, care, and attention. Such food tastes delicious, it is healthy, and digestion is easy.

Where there is simplicity, there is authenticity. Simple clothes are clothes which keep you warm or keep you cool according to the season. But when you buy clothes because of a designer label, you lose simplicity. You go to a big fancy shop, and you pay a huge sum for a shirt which you can buy in a simple shop much more cheaply. With a designer label, you are paying for the name and glamor, not for the shirt. This is dressing the ego rather than the body. Sometimes it is called "power dressing."

Often shopping becomes a habit, and in order to maintain this habit, we have to work hard to earn more money, to buy more things, and then finally we put them in the attic and forget them.

Achieving external simplicity can be easier if we work at the same time on internal simplicity. Simplicity of thought and mind will lead to a reduction of the desire for material things. The opposite of a simple state of mind is to be possessed by ambition for name, fame, prestige, and power. Ego makes our lives and minds complicated. How do *I* get power? How can *I* become famous? We become obsessed by such questions.

Simplicity leads to humility. Humility leads to right relationship, right communication, right understanding, and right appreciation. These are soul qualities. If we do not wish to complicate our lives, then we have to shift from *ego* to *eco*. Ego separates and eco connects. Ego complicates, eco simplifies. *Eco* means "home" where relationships are nurtured. When we get stuck in our ego, we get disconnected from others.

Elegant simplicity practiced at every level—physical, material, mental, and spiritual—is the key. When we make our lives simple at all levels, then we can live in freedom. Clearing of emotional, mental, and material clutter is essential for freedom.

There is even a National Simplicity Day now, July 12, described as "a time to take a step back and begin to simplify our lives." Its proponents suggest that one "start by slowing down, tuning into nature, enjoying the simple things in life, decluttering, and striving for balance. Once you have done this, you can begin to enjoy the many stress-reducing pleasures and benefits of a simple lifestyle."

We can learn simplicity from Nature. We plant a seed,

then the soil, the rain, and the sunshine work together and that seed becomes a tree. The tree has branches, blossoms, leaves, and fruit. Then autumn comes, and all the leaves fall, giving nutrition to the soil. In the winter, the tree rests and sleeps, it hibernates. Then spring comes, and it is exuberant again. The tree is not ambitious, a tree doesn't want to be something more than it is, a tree wants to be a tree, that is all. An apple tree wants to be an apple tree and is just happy to be one. It doesn't need to be more or less. Whatever it is, it is. In our lives, we too can be ourselves, without ambition, anxiety, ego, or desire. Without striving for something which we are not.

Shakespeare's Hamlet questions, "To be or not to be?" The answer we are still looking for is to be who we are. To be ourselves. I am. I am myself. The journey of self-discovery is a journey towards simplicity, it is a journey to the source. From the source, water flows, tributaries form. Family, friends, and colleagues come. Everything joins the great river of life. Such simplicity leads to a life of abundance.

Spirituality helps us to be simple. Materialism is complicated. Materialism involves accumulating and possessing. Status is judged by possessions. Kings and Queens have palaces and castles. They have a huge amount of land, staff, and servants. It is difficult for them to lead a simple life. Similarly the life of many nouveau riche billionaires cannot be simple either. They have many houses, staff, and advisors. They are under a great deal of pressure and cannot do what they really want to do. They are almost imprisoned. Now that President Obama has left the White House, he may have more freedom to do what he wants to do, say what he wants to say, and write what he wants to write.

Before he became president, he wrote a wonderful book, *The Audacity of Hope*. But once he became president, he lost some of that audacity and hope.

If we take the example of spiritual leaders like Jesus Christ, the Buddha, St. Francis, Mother Teresa, Martin Luther King, and Mahatma Gandhi, we will find that they were all free spirits. They lived very simple lives. Mahatma Gandhi wore a loin cloth and spun his own clothes. He had one shawl for the winter and in summer was half naked. When he traveled by train, he went third class. Once somebody asked him, "Why do you travel third class, Mr. Gandhi?" He answered, "I travel in the third class because there is no fourth class!" He was a great example of simplicity by being close to people, being natural, being ordinary. To be ordinary is the most extraordinary thing we can do in our lives. By being ordinary, we drop our ego and our desire to have someone admire us. We are not dependent on somebody else's judgment. If somebody is judging you or criticizing you, then that is their affair. If they think that because you don't have a big enough house or car therefore you are not successful, then that is their perception. It's not your problem. We want to live our lives simply and joyfully, that is what matters. As long as we are comfortable in ourselves, that is enough.

In our educational system, we are judged by teachers. Then in a job interview, we are judged again. Someone decides who is good, who is better, and who is no good at all. We are conditioned to present ourselves to be judged by somebody—by our parents, by our teachers, by our employers, or by our colleagues. Self-knowledge gives us strength so that we do not wish to be judged by others or measured by the shallow standards of the market. We need to apply our own standards and our own vision in order to celebrate the fundamental dignity of human life.

Self-awareness, self-acceptance, and self-appreciation are part of a simple life. When we are free of expectations, we are free of disappointment. Simplicity has no formula or technique. Each of us has to find our own way; there is no rule which everyone must follow. It is a lifelong process with no final destination. We don't need to worry about when we are going to achieve a perfect state of simplicity. We are on a journey, a pilgrimage. Day after day, focus on simplicity of mind, thought, speech, feeling, action, food, clothes, house, intention, and relationships. With constant attention, we grow into a natural and unselfconscious state of simplicity.

We need to recognize that our brain is made up of two hemispheres. The left hemisphere is rational, ambitious, and calculating. The right hemisphere deals with imagination, intuition, feelings, and spirit. In a state of elegant simplicity, these two hemispheres come together in balance and harmony.

Simplicity is not only of the external, it is also of the internal. We are always engaged in making and doing, thinking and feeling. In all these activities, we need to cultivate implicit and explicit simplicity. How to be simple while cooking, gardening, taking a shower, or making the bed? We need to do every action, from small to large, with a light touch, a small footprint. The moment we make heavy weather of things, life becomes more complicated. Simplicity means we flow through life as a river flows through a landscape.

Complexity is not the same as complication. Complexity is natural and beautiful. Simplicity and complexity are complementary. Our bodies are very complex, the microorganisms and bacteria in our bodies are complex. Yet the body is also very simple. We all manage our bodies quite well. We eat, we shower, we wash, we go to the toilet, and we sleep; we do everything in a simple way and manage this complex structure. We do not need a PhD to look after our bodies.

Existence is complex, yet simple. Academics and economists make it complicated. For example, the process of weaving a carpet is complex and intricate. All the threads and colors are woven together, yet a traditional weaver produces a complex piece of work without a university degree. With attention and awareness, carpet weavers make the complex simple.

This simplicity is rooted in consciousness, which means "knowing together." Consciousness connects us with past, present, and future, with our ancestors and future generations, with time and space, with matter and spirit. Consciousness is the ground of our elegantly simple relationship with the universe. In Hindu philosophy, consciousness is the primary principle. The universe and all our actions within it emerge out of consciousness. Sun, moon, stars, planets, galaxies, trees, oceans, mountains, animals, and humans are all manifestations of consciousness. The complex question of origin has a simple answer. This invisible consciousness manifests itself in visible forms. Consciousness is the ultimate reality. Consciousness is the cosmic mind. The intimate human mind is linked to the ultimate universal mind. From ultimate to intimate and vice versa, there is no gap, no disconnect. We could call this cosmic mind the mind of

God, within which everything merges and submerges. And emerges again. In this cosmic reality, there is an implicit order. What looks like chaos is in fact orderly. This order maintains trillions of life forms, big and small. It has great simplicity.

We should not be afraid of chaos in our lives. Out of our fear of chaos, we have developed complicated systems. Our lives are now controlled by the clock, the diary, appointments. My mother had no clock. At night she knew the time by looking at the stars. Her life was simple. My life is complicated in comparison. She had a bit of a wild mind. I have become timid and organized. My garden is manicured. The lawn, the trees, the flowers are organized. That may seem like order, but it lacks the quality of *wabi sabi*. There is a paradox here: what may appear as disorder has implicit order, and what appears as order is complicated. A forest appears chaotic, but there is implicit order, self-organized and self-maintained. The life of my mother and the life of the forest resemble each other.

The practice of simplicity requires spontaneity and improvisation. For example, when somebody comes to my door, if I am a slave to my diary, I will say, "You didn't make an appointment, I can't see you now, I'm busy." My mother would never say this. In the Indian tradition, the word for guest is *atithi* which means "one who comes without appointment." In every situation, we need to allow for the unplanned, the unexpected event, we need to be flexible and spontaneous. We need to improvise. Things cannot all be written down. New things are always emerging. We have to be able to embrace the emergent situation. When something new occurs, let's welcome it. There's a type of music in Pakistan called Qawwali. It is improvised. There is a lead singer and some supporting singers; a constant conversation goes on between them. There is an element of the wild in this music. Indian classical music is also improvised. There are no written notes. My mother would say that life is like music. There are scales, there are patterns, but there is no score. Life asks us to play and improvise.

Spontaneity and improvisation free us from worries. Worrying dissipates our energy. We need to cultivate a habit of not worrying. Why worry about the past? We need to let go of the past. We don't need to worry about the future either. Khalil Gibran said, "Yesterday is but today's memory, tomorrow is today's dream." Only the present is real. That is why it is called "present"—a gift. We need to respond to the situation in which we find ourselves. There is a formula for this: 10 percent of thinking can be concerned with the past, 15 percent with the future, and the remaining 75 percent with the present. When we live mostly in the present, we can move easily, step by step. We can respond to events with an open heart and an open mind. Worrying about the past or the future saps our energy, and we can't respond fully to the situation in front of us. The present moment is the potent moment. Let's live it as well as we can!

To do this we need to trust. Trust that we are capable of dealing with the future when it arrives. We don't have to worry about it now. We need not anticipate problems. They may or may not arise. We have the potential to deal with the future, whatever it may hold, good or bad, negative or positive. We have imagination, we have ability. Remember, whatever we plan, that plan may not work out. So why do so much planning? Just have a little bit of an idea of the future. If we have excessive planning and the plan doesn't work out, we will be disappointed.

Instead of so much planning, let us have vision. A vision is like a dream. Let the planning evolve step by step from your vision. Let the future emerge as it will. As Joseph Campbell said, "We must let go of the life we have planned, so as to accept the one that is waiting for us." Not being fixed and dogmatic with plans has its own magic, its own energy. When we allow things to emerge, miracles can happen. When we plan too much in advance, miracles may be blocked. When everything is planned, there is no room for something new to emerge. It is easier to embrace simplicity when we follow the way of minimal planning and maximum improvisation.

The meaning of elegant simplicity goes deep and has nothing to do with harsh austerity, scarcity, deprivation, or self-denial. It may seem paradoxical, but the gift of simplicity is the gift of abundance. When we know enough is enough, we have more than enough. Simplicity offers sufficiency over extravagance, comfort over convenience, contentment over cravings, reconciliation over resentment.

Richard Gregg, a friend of Mahatma Gandhi, called it *voluntary simplicity*. It means sincerity and honesty within as well as the reduction of material clutter without; it means avoidance of many possessions irrelevant to the chief purpose of life; it means restraint in some directions in order to secure greater abundance of life in other directions such as having time to pursue music, poetry, gardening, time for friends, etc.

We can realize this all-embracing vision of elegant simplicity in our lives by avoiding mass production and mass consumption. William Morris translated this vision through the arts and crafts movement, through the manifestation of imagination by working, making, and producing simple but elegant objects for everyday use. I will consider this aspect of simplicity in the next chapter.

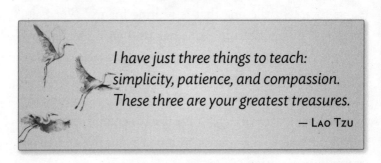

I have just three things to teach: simplicity, patience, and compassion. These three are your greatest treasures.

— Lao Tzu

a society of artists

This world is but a canvas
to our imagination.

Henry David Thoreau

Once upon a time in India, many people studied many of the 64 arts of living, if not all, which included the art of preparing a bed for the night, washing your body, decorating your body, making love (Kama Sutra), caring for the family, lighting a fire, worshipping in the temple, breathing, meditation, singing, dancing, painting, building a house, growing food, cooking, making furniture, and many more.

By cultivating these 64 arts and skillful means of operating in the world, students learned to meet their physical needs as well as their emotional, intellectual, and spiritual needs. No distinction was made between those arts which fulfill spiritual needs and those which fulfill emotional or physical needs.

When we make a pot or a sculpture, we are making ourselves. When we cultivate the soil, we also cultivate the soul. While we grow food in the field, we also cultivate patience within ourselves. The inner arts and the outer arts are two aspects of one single reality. The arts of making and the arts of being complement each other and bring us a sense of fulfillment, contentment, and satisfaction. To be an artist is to be a maker and vice versa.

When we have participated in the process of making, only then are we entitled to consume. In such a paradigm, which transforms employees and consumers into makers and artists, people will work in cooperatives, free of hierarchies. Relationship will replace the idea of ownership. Such

a system will not consider humans as owners of natural resources. Natural resources are there as a gift. We humans
would receive these gifts with gratitude, use them with
care, and share them, not only with all the members of the
human community but with all living beings of the Earth
community.

Artists do not seek employment or jobs, they seek right
livelihood, and thus the human footprint upon the living
Earth is light. When society is made up of artists, then the
purpose of the economy becomes the fulfillment of the
genuine needs of everyone and not the false greed of a few.
There is enough for everybody's need but not for anybody's
greed. There is an abundance of everything because Nature is abundant. In the society of artists, there is no waste
and no pollution, just as there is neither waste nor pollution in Nature. Whatever gifts artists receive from Nature
they return back to Nature. All the activities of artists are
regenerative and renewable. I dream of a society of artists
who, above all, practice the art of living. By cultivating the
arts of living, we can make our lives more simple, more
harmonious, more joyful, and more contented.

When we make something by hand, we unselfconsciously
create beauty. Because we have left to one side the art of
making by hand, we have surrounded ourselves with ugliness. The industrial mode of mass production has created
an ugly civilization. We are ruled by numbers, obsessed
by the economy, and possessed by speed—all enemies of
beauty. A monster is haunting the modern world, the monster of ugly materialism. The goddess of beauty has van-
ished from the house of humanity. When we are bereft of

beauty, we are also bereft of truth. "Beauty is truth, truth beauty," as the English poet Keats wrote. The absence of beauty and truth is at the root of the decadence of our time.

Only art, which means making by hand, can cure the problems of humanity. Art can wash away the ugliness of our civilization. It is art that can defeat the forces of materialism and restore the rule of beauty. It is art that can reveal the secrets of the imagination and free us from the bondage of greed, speed, and clutter. "The ecological crisis is a crisis of aesthetics," stated the late James Hillman, an American psychologist. By restoring aesthetics, we restore ecological balance.

But sadly, even art has fallen into the hands of the smart and the slick. Throw elephant dung on a picture of the Virgin Mary and you become a famous artist. Put your unmade bed in the Tate gallery and sell it as a work of art for a large sum of money. This shows how the sickness of civilization has permeated all spheres of life. Art has been hijacked by entertainers and moneymakers.

We have forgotten the wisdom of Henry James who said, "It is art that makes life." We have separated art from everyday living and imprisoned it in galleries and museums. Now is the time to liberate art from sensationalism and commercialism and restore integrity, authenticity, and meaning to it.

According to Ananda Coomaraswamy, "An artist is not a special kind of person but every person is a special kind of artist." Homemaking, cooking, dancing, singing, and gardening are some of the art forms that we neglect at our peril. In the Kama Sutra, it is considered essential for a good lover—man or woman—to learn the 64 arts of living and loving. How can you please your beloved if you don't know how to grow flowers and arrange them attractively beside your bed?

Not only does artist mean maker, the word *poet* also means "maker," as in *autopoesis*, a Greek term meaning "self-created." Poetry is not only imaginative words on a page; every imaginative act is a poem. *Poeisis* was first a verb, not a noun, indicating an action which transforms the world. Poetic work reconciles thought with matter and time, and people with the world—a beautiful vision of unity through making.

Nature is God's poetry, God's art. God acts through a gardener, who creates her garden as art. Similarly, producing solar energy, organizing the economy, or running a school are also art forms. Art is a state of mind. When we do something well, without being distracted by desire for fame, fortune, or power, then our work becomes a work of art. Scientists, politicians, and business people become artists when they perform their work with love and imagination. James Lovelock, originator of Gaia theory, once said to me, "I practice science as an artist. I don't follow orders from governments or corporations. I follow my intuition, my inspiration, and above all my imagination." The sculptor and land artist Richard Long told me, "I walk as an artist." Thus walking mindfully becomes an art form.

Some time ago, I visited an aboriginal community in Australia. I asked them, "What is your work? How do you earn your livelihood?" They replied, "We are all artists here." I was delighted! How many communities in the world can make this claim?

Once Bertrand Russell visited an indigenous village in Africa. During the day, people worked in the fields. In the evening, they had a simple meal, mostly millet and a bit of meat with some homemade wine. In comparison to Russell's usual three-course dinner, this was very basic. Then they started to sing. They kept singing. Then they began to dance. Russell looked at his watch. The villagers had no watches, but Russell did. It was 10 o'clock at night. Then 11 o'clock, then midnight. His hosts kept singing and dancing, they were happy and enjoying themselves. Russell had never come across such joy. No one there was worried about world problems. These tribal people had few if any mental or physical problems, and they were unaware of lacking material possessions. Russell said, "I wish I'd been born here, free of my anguish and anxieties!"

Indigenous cultures have no word for art as we understand it in the Western world. For them, something made well, with imagination and skill, is art, without naming it as such. For them, art is part of everyday life. But our utilitarian and industrial civilization has taken the arts out of everyday life. Art has become a luxury. Painting, drawing, dancing, singing, and acting are not something most of us do as part of everyday life. We practice them either as a hobby, or they become the profession of a privileged few. But the art of living is the greatest art. *Art* means "to make or manifest with imagination, with creativity, and with your heart." There is a close relationship between every kind of art, whether fine art or crafts.

In indigenous cultures, art is neither a hobby nor a luxury, but an essential ingredient of everyday living and being. Artworks are found not in museums or galleries but in homes and fields, as objects of daily use. Indigenous art shows a combination of skill and loving attention. Making with love means surrendering to the materials and the process. There is no holding back. This kind of work lets go of control and allows something to emerge. Skill comes through regular practice, when day after day the makers devote themselves to their work. Mindful making is like meditation. The mind has to be fully present in the moment of making. Thus, arts and crafts are ways of celebrating life, community, culture, and Nature. There is neither hierarchy nor division between arts and crafts.

We have moved so far from this understanding of art. In the modern world, the artist has become more important than the art of making. In the Middle Ages, art was created for "God's sake." Later art came to be practiced for "man's sake." The modern age promoted the idea of art for "art's sake," and in post-modern times, when conceptual art rules, art is for the "artist's sake." I have difficulty in calling something "art" if it involves no skill, no beauty, and not much making. Why not call it "concept" rather than corrupt the much loved ideal of art? Art cannot be divorced from integrity, from truth, from beauty, from life. Art is not merely a concept, it is a way of life.

The divorce of art from life began when artists started to claim a higher status than artisans, separating themselves from their fellow craftsmen and women. When art became a status symbol, it became disconnected from ordinary life. Art grew apart, to be practiced only by those with "special" talents, and to be purchased only by those with great wealth. Thus art became one more item of consumption, a commodity to be bought and sold, an object for investment, and no longer a way of life practiced by everyone as an everyday activity.

We are at the cusp of a new revolution, a new awakening, where we wish to reinstate the relationship between art and the land we live on, the clothes we wear, and the things we make. A new movement of artists like Andy Goldsworthy, Susan Derges, Richard Long, Chris Druery, Sandy Brown, and others is emerging, where life, Nature, and art are a seamless continuum. When art is part of everyone's life, it can heal the wounds of the soul inflicted by an ugly civilization of clutter and consumption.

Only through reconnecting culture with Nature, utility with beauty, making with consuming, and art with craft can we stride towards freedom from the tyranny of money, materialism, and mass production.

Art has transformative power. Artists are alchemists. They transform base material into objects of beauty, utility, and delight. Potters take a lump of ordinary clay and reveal its extraordinary ability to be a pot of pure visual pleasure as well as a vessel to fulfill everyday functions of holding water and wine, food and flowers. Painters take pigments of red, blue, and yellow of no great distinction, put them on a pot or on paper, on a wall or on canvas, and a delightful work of art emerges, be it folk art or fine art.

The materials used by the vast number of potters, painters, sculptors, and basket makers are often inexpensive, natural, and locally available. It is the power of patience and practice, the power of imagination and endurance, the power of hands, feet, and voice, and ultimately the power of the human spirit, which transform willow wands into baskets, stone into sculptures, wood into wardrobes, sound into songs, and words into poems. The joy of it is that we are all potential alchemists. We are all capable of becoming artists and artisans.

As the maker transforms clay into a pot, the clay transforms the maker into a potter. The capacity of clay to transform ordinary and unformed humans into evolved and self-realized sages like Bernard Leach and Lucie Rie is magnificent. If there were no clay, there would be no famous potter like Michael Cardew; if there were no paint, there would be no Picasso; if there were no flowers, there would be no Vincent van Gogh or Georgia O'Keeffe. As the artist is an alchemist, transforming the ordinary into the extraordinary, so too does the material bring about the metamorphosis of the maker. As we adore the maker, we also need to respect and adore the material. By doing so, we go beyond the division between fine arts and folk arts, between artist and artisan. It is always the intimacy between the maker and their material which reveals imagination, creativity, and spontaneity.

Art is not a profession, it is a form of right livelihood where profession and vocation merge. An economy founded on arts and crafts is a resilient economy, indeed a peace economy. The sooner we embrace the arts and crafts as an integral part of our economic life, the sooner we will be able to address the environmental and spiritual malaise of our time. An economy of mass production and mass consumption is a never-ending rat race which leads to boundless discontent, with little sense of the fulfillment and satisfaction that can be derived from making things by hand.

The anxiety, meaninglessness, and depression from which a large number of people suffer is caused by a lack of creativity. Modern industrial civilization is the enemy of the imagination. It is the destroyer of arts, crafts, culture, and creativity for the majority of people. The minority which perseveres in practicing the arts and crafts struggle to survive or are forced to commercialize their art and seek celebrity status.

Being an employee is in stark contrast to being an artist. A society where everyone can be an artist has to be organized in a totally different way from that of modern society. In the present system, the economy rules, not the imagination and creativity. The economy requires us to be consumers of mass-produced goods in order to accelerate economic growth. A society founded on the idea of everyone being an artist requires us to become makers and producers so that we can achieve personal, social, and ecological well-being. The economy, in this ideal system, is the servant of humanity and not the master. In my worldview, a life of elegant simplicity would be built on a firm foundation of the arts and crafts. We need to move away from automation, industrialism, and robotic systems. We need to embrace the ideal of mindful making.

When mindful making is the basis for our civilization, then working with the arts and crafts becomes a spiritual practice. We honor the material world and while doing so develop a sense of the sacred. In Indian culture, this is called karma yoga, the yoga of action. In the next chapter, I will elucidate the meaning of this vital and visionary practice. The way of elegant simplicity is a natural consequence of karma yoga.

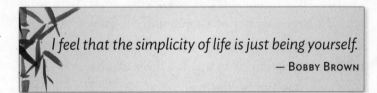

I feel that the simplicity of life is just being yourself.
— Bobby Brown

yoga of action

Life is a process,
not a product.
Brian Goodwin

ONE OF THE MOST powerful teachings of Hinduism is that of karma yoga, which instructs us to act without desiring the fruit of our action. To the Western mind, which is so result oriented, this may seem an impossible idea, but if we look deeply, there is much wisdom and simplicity in it. This teaching has far-reaching implications and a radical effect on daily life. It has evolved over thousands of years, and many Hindu philosophers, sages, and practitioners have contributed to its evolution. They have called it the master idea.

Before exploring the yoga of action, let me write a few words about Hinduism to give a context to the teaching. Hinduism takes its name from a river locally known as the river Hindu (the Indus). The river Indus has given its name to the country, India in English and Hindustan in Hindi, to many of its people, Hindus, and their language, Hindi. The river, considered to be sacred, comes from Mount Kailash, a sacred source in the Himalayas. The river runs through Ladakh, Kashmir, and then Pakistan, where it flows south to the Arabian Sea. A few centuries ago, when people from the west crossed the river, they found a country of thirty-six thousand deities where people worshipped gods and goddesses of rivers, mountains, and forests. Foreign travelers called this form of worship "Hinduism."

Hinduism is made up of six formal philosophies and many informal ones. Some of the most profound Hindu thinking is encapsulated in the Upanishads, which means to "sit at the feet of a spiritual master and engage in dialogue." This was an oral culture. Texts were memorized and learned by heart. The Upanishads tend to be short. One of them is the *Ishavashyopanishad* which has only 18 verses. The first verse encapsulates the belief that the natural elements, the earth, air, water, and fire are sacred. There is no other god than the god within each and every living being. There is no separate god beyond this Earth, this universe, and this cosmos in some faraway heaven.

Everything that we see, touch, feel, sense, smell, or hear is sacred. Whatever is in the universe is divine. The Upanishads praise the generosity of the Earth. They remind us that the seed of the banyan tree is the smallest of seeds and yet produces the biggest tree. In the botanical garden of Calcutta, there is the great banyan tree with a thousand branches. It is so large that people call it the "one tree forest." The tree covers nearly five acres of land. This tree is a beautiful example of the Earth's abundance and her sacred nature.

The *Ishavashyopanishad* says, "Enjoy the fruits of the Earth." Not only humans but every creature is invited to enjoy the gifts of the Earth, but on one condition—take only your share and leave some for others, so that they can also enjoy the fruit.

In the apple season, there are so many apples on the tree that birds, wasps and bees, and even the earthworms can eat them. The soil feeds and nourishes the apple tree, then the fallen apples nourish the soil. This is the sacred cycle of Nature.

The Hindu perspective on life and nature is not linear, it is cyclical. As we saw when talking about pilgrimage, life is an eternal journey, without a goal, without a destination. Therefore we shouldn't focus on the outcome of our action, we should focus on the action itself.

The *Bhagavad Gita* is another significant Upanishad. Many Sanskrit scholars learn it by heart. My teacher, Vinoba Bhave, was one of them. During the struggle for Indian independence, he was imprisoned by the British. There were a few hundred political prisoners in jail with him. They asked Vinoba to teach them the essence of the Gita. Vinoba said, "I will, but you have to get permission from the prison governor." A deputation went to the governor who agreed that a large meeting could take place weekly in the jail, for Vinoba to give a discourse on the Gita. Then the governor asked, "Can I also come and hear Vinoba?"

"Of course you can" said the prisoners. Thus in Dhulia jail in Maharashtra, Vinoba gave his talks on the Gita. One of the prisoners was a journalist who wrote down the talks word for word in shorthand. This was later published as *Talks on the Gita*. Many of my own spiritual and ecological insights have been significantly inspired by these *Talks*.

The Gita is a long poem, an allegory of war and peace. It takes place during a bitter struggle between members of one large family. On one side there are a hundred brothers and on the other side are their five cousins. They fight for control of the kingdom. The Gita is that part of the epic *Mahabharata* in which Lord Krishna is in dialogue with the warrior Arjuna who has doubts about a war in which he is required to fight members of his own family. The author uses the concept of war as a metaphor for action. He points out that war is a consequence of the desire to control, to conquer, and to gain power. By overcoming these human desires, we can overcome conflicts and wars.

It is also a struggle between two aspects of human nature, one constructive and the other destructive.

When the *Bhagavad Gita* was written, there was a movement in India encouraging people to renounce the world. The Buddha, Mahavir, and many of their followers were from the princely and landowning classes, and they were joining monastic orders. The Gita was written to counteract this movement. Krishna says to Arjuna, "Renounce attachment to the world but do not forsake the world. Do not renounce action in the world."

Thus the Gita presents the philosophy of karma yoga in the clearest and most profound manner. It argues that action is natural to all human beings and impossible to avoid. We all need to act. Our body is made to act. If anyone is asked to sit in a room and told, don't do anything, just sit here for a week or a month and do nothing, that person would not be happy. Our natural urge is to move, to garden, to cook, to make, to build, to plant, to sing, and to dance. Action is our natural source of fulfillment. Action is beautiful. Action is its own reward, a source of pleasure and joy. The Gita urges us to participate and be fully engaged in action without worrying about the result. When we do not desire the result, nor hanker for praise and achievement, then our focus is fully on our action which should be as perfect and complete as possible. If we act with pure intentions, then it will be yogic action and it will not have harmful consequences. Action without yoga is like a sticky glue. The glue is desire for and attachment to achievement. The wish for praise or recognition is a glue which will attract karmic consequences. If we do not desire the fruit of our action, then we are liberated from self-importance and from ego. The Gita says, "Never renounce action, renounce the desire for the fruit of action. Never renounce the world, renounce attachment to the world."

Our action should be an offering in the service of others and not for personal gain. When somebody is ill, or somebody is old or hungry, if we don't act, how will we help them? So act in mutuality, in reciprocity, in service, with love, with care, with compassion and kindness. Every action is a form of service. Gardening is a form of service. We are serving not only our nearest and dearest, we are caring for and replenishing the earth itself. We are cultivating the soil, and when we cultivate the soil, we also cultivate our soul. As we remove weeds from the garden, we also remove the weeds of anxiety, anger, pride, ego, and fear from our lives. By being at one with the soil, we reconnect with the elements. Thus gardening becomes yoga of action, a spiritual practice, a mediation.

Karma yoga becomes a way of life. Every action that we perform with attention and mindfulness, free from craving and clinging, is karma yoga. Cooking, gardening, writing a book, building a house, making furniture, walking by the river, whatever we are doing if we are fully present in the here and now, then it is karma yoga. This is the Hindu ideal of action. As we saw in the previous chapter, an artist focuses on the process of making rather than the outcome. Be it singing, dancing, or painting, the action is complete in itself. Any results and outcomes are inconsequential. Thus a karma yogi is an artist in the truest sense.

According to the Gita, karma yoga is the basis of our spirituality. In the spirituality of the Gita, there is no dogma, no church, no mosque, no temple, no holy book. There is no separation between being spiritual and being active in the world. There is no separation between God and the world. In karma yoga, the gap between the outer and the inner world is bridged. The inner landscape of love and the outer landscape of Nature are one. Without inner there is no outer. Walls make the room; if there are no walls, there is no room. The temple may be a reminder of the sacred, it may help us in our search for a spiritual path, but it is not where spirituality resides; spirituality resides in our hearts. The Gita challenged the notion that living in a monastic order is more pure than living in the world. If our heart is pure and our intentions good, then we can live happily and simply in the world. That was the reason I felt compelled to leave the monastic order and be in the world and practice spirituality in everyday life.

Whereas the Gita presented the philosophy and the vision that all actions conducted with right intention and without attachment constitute the yoga of action, the Jains argued that right intention is not enough. The yoga of action must always be nonviolent. A violent action undertaken even with right intention is not yoga.

At that time in the Hindu temples of India, there was ritual sacrifice of animals. The intention was that people should not kill an animal unless it was for food, and if they really needed to kill an animal for food, they should first offer it to the gods. It had become a custom for people to take an animal to the temple for slaughter, make an offering to the deities, and then to feast. The argument was that in making an offering to the gods, with pure intention, the killing of animals became acceptable. In the same way, the Gita said a war fought with pure intention was justified. The Jain teacher, Mahavir, countered that purity of intent was not enough. The action itself must also be pure and nonviolent. Noble ends should always be carried out with noble means. This is why the metaphor of war used in the Gita is not acceptable to Jains. Thus Mahavir became a campaigner for compassion to animals and to all living beings. By doing so, he added a new dimension to the ideal of karma yoga.

Mahavir advocated a reformed karma yoga. Yes, renounce the desire for the fruit of your action, but also renounce any trace of violence in your action. He proposed that everyone should be vegetarian. Although Hindus recognized certain animals as sacred, such as cows, bulls, monkeys, peacocks, and swans, they allowed themselves ritual killing of other animals at an altar in the temple. Mahavir praised them for their concept of the sacred cow but urged them to extend that sense of the sacred to all living beings.

For Mahavir the practice of nonviolence is the essential quality of a karma yogi. It also included nonviolence of the mind. People should avoid negative, violent, malicious, or harmful thoughts. Speech should also be nonviolent. When we speak, we should use kind words. If we have to speak a difficult truth, speak it sweetly, and if we cannot speak the truth sweetly, then we should keep silence and wait until we have learned to speak the truth sweetly and nonviolently.

Mahavir established a tradition of pacifism, and Jains were the first pacifists of India. Sixteen hundred years ago, some Jain monks came to the village of Os where my ancestors lived. They preached the practice of complete nonviolence. The villagers, including my ancestors, were so inspired that they decided to become Jains. Some of them were soldiers of the king. They had to ask the king's permission to become pacifists. These Jains set the example of conscientious objection. The king permitted them to change from the warrior caste to the merchant caste. The doctrine of the Jains was in complete contrast to the doctrine of the Gita. For Jains there is no just war. There is no place for any war, even as a metaphor.

Jains practice nonviolence to people but also nonviolence to Nature. They do not cut trees. They do not dig the soil, and they will not grow or eat root vegetables like potatoes, onions, garlic, carrots, or beetroot, because by harvesting the roots they would be tearing the soil apart. So they only take that part of the crop which is above the ground. Jains would prefer to be fruitarians, or to eat those vegetables that are the fruit of the plant such as beans and peas. When legumes and grains are picked, the roots are left in the soil, and then when they die naturally, they become part of the soil. Thus for Jains living simply means living nonviolently and frugally.

Mahatma Gandhi took the philosophy of karma yoga even further. He embodied both Hindu and Jain traditions. His father was a Hindu, and his mother was a Jain. The Mahatma introduced social, political, and economic karma yoga. He argued that the modern economy, the factory system, industrialization, mass production and mechanization, the destruction of craft and artwork, are all violence. If people make things with their hands, then there is minimum use of transport, minimum use of fossil fuels and other natural resources, and this makes for a simpler, more elegant, and nonviolent way of living.

Similarly, centralized and militarized big government is also a form of violence because it takes power away from ordinary people. Gandhi's karma yoga advocates politics on a human scale and decentralized power. For him small was always beautiful. Thus Gandhi represents a synthesis of the Hindu ideal of action and the Hindu art of living, which entails detachment from goal-oriented and results-bound activities, and the Jain values of nonviolence in thought, speech, and action. Building on these two spiritual traditions, Gandhi developed a new system of karma yoga that included right action in the political and economic sphere, as well as in the personal sphere.

Gandhi's karma yoga agreed with the Jains that noble ends must be pursued by noble means. There should be no contradiction between ends and means. Purity of intention and purity of action go hand in hand. The ideal and the pragmatic need to be congruent. This means acting with right motivation, with nonviolent means, and in the service of humanity and the Earth. A karma yogi must avoid actions which damage social cohesion and natural harmony.

These three aspects of karma yoga, brought together, form the ideal basis for elegant simplicity.

The concept and practice of karma yoga, however, appears to be idealistic and beyond our reach. We are thoroughly conditioned to be goal oriented. Where do we start to decondition ourselves? How do we create a society of artists and karma yogis? How do we start the process of elegant simplicity? In my view, we have to begin at the beginning, with childhood and schools. So in the next chapter, let us turn to questions of education and learning.

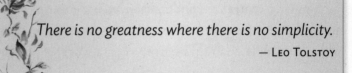

There is no greatness where there is no simplicity.
— LEO TOLSTOY

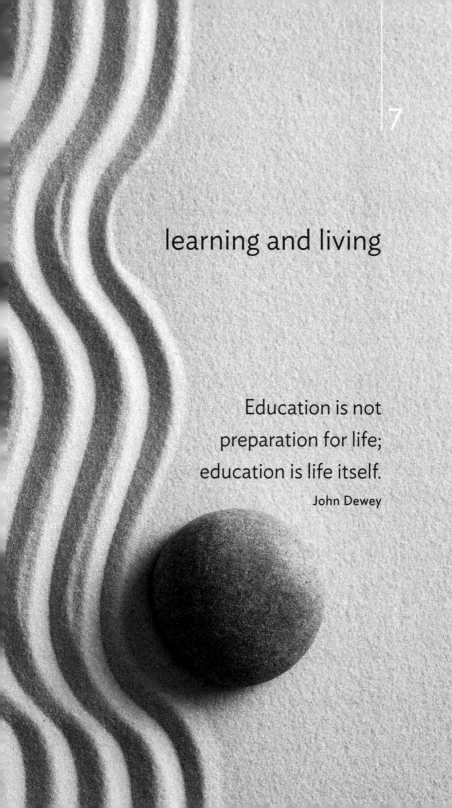

learning and living

Education is not
preparation for life;
education is life itself.

John Dewey

Simplicity has to begin in the beginning. It has to begin in childhood. A child is like a seed. With the right conditions, the seed has the potential to become that which is inside it. An acorn becomes an oak, an apple seed becomes an apple tree. The work of a gardener, a forester, or a farmer is not to make an oak into an ash, or an apple into a pear. But when a child goes to school, teachers need to understand the qualities of the child: "Is this child an apple or a pear?"

But unfortunately, in modern schools teachers seldom observe the qualities of the child. Children are required to fit into an economic system. Children have to become what the economy requires. The government says, "We need engineers, bankers, economists, accountants, doctors." The schools train children to meet the needs of the market and prepare them to get good jobs, become successful and earn as much as possible so that they can accumulate as many material gadgets and possessions as possible. But in an ideal and proper education system, children would not be made to suit the economy, rather the economy would be made to suit the child. Moreover, children should be prepared for a life which is fulfilling and happy.

I did not like the modern model of education, so I started a school in Hartland, North Devon, in 1982. My two children were of the age to go to secondary school, and it would have been in a town 15 miles away. They would have to travel by bus one hour in the morning and one hour in the evening, every day. A commuter's life starting at the age of eleven! I didn't want my children to have to endure those journeys. My wife and I had moved from a city to live in a village because we wanted to live in a rural community, and we wanted our children to grow up in a rural environment. We wanted them to learn from Nature, from forests, from the flora and fauna. We wanted them to know about the lives of farmers and builders, painters and poets. If every morning at eight o'clock they had to go away from our rural community to a faraway town and come back exhausted in the evening, then they could not develop an understanding for or a relationship with their community. From high school, they would go on to university which would train them to be useful to the economy. Then they would look for a well-paid job somewhere in London, Paris, New York, or New Delhi. Thus, like other young people, our children would be taken away from their village and uprooted from their community.

We did not want our children to be educated away from our community. So I called a meeting in the village. I was delighted that about 30 people came. After some preliminary discussion, I asked them, "What do you think of bussing our children to the town for schooling?" Parents replied, "Some children smoke on the bus. Some of them are bullied. There is no supervision. We need a school in our village."

After an hour of discussion, the parents of nine children said, "If you start a school in Hartland, we will send our children to it." According to British law, a school can be recognized and registered with only five children—and we had nine! So we started The Small School.

The very first day, when nine children and their parents came to the school, we asked, "How is our school going to be different from any other school? The answer was, "Most children will walk to school. The kitchen will be a classroom. Every day children will participate in cooking. There will be real, fresh food to eat for lunch. They will bake fresh bread every day. There will be a garden where children will learn to grow vegetables, herbs, and flowers. Why do schools have football and cricket fields but no gardens? Every school should have a garden and a kitchen."

In many schools in the UK, food is prepared miles away by a contractor and then driven to the school. Why? All children should learn to cook healthy and nutritious food. They should learn the history of food, the chemistry and mathematics of food. We said, "We are not going to teach only Shakespeare, Darwin, Newton, and Galileo, we are going to teach cooking, gardening, building, sewing, mending, woodwork, photography, and music in addition to maths, science, and English." This was our curriculum. Our school was not going to be an exam factory, it was to be a place of self-discovery.

Of course, we had developed these ideas over a period of a few months during which the parents, teachers, and potential students themselves were involved in discussions. When, on the first day, I articulated these ideas, everyone was happy to hear them.

We are all in favor of knowledge, but it should be accompanied by experience. Physics, chemistry, mathematics, evolution, philosophy, psychology, theology—these are just words. Real knowledge is beyond words. Beyond theories and concepts. Real understanding comes from experience.

So our school would incorporate knowledge with lived experience. The Small School curriculum included arts, crafts, stories, and myths as much as science and maths.

The Small School lasted for 36 years as a full-time school, but a new state-funded school with some of the same ideals as The Small School has now started in the area. Parents can now send their children there without having to pay any fees. However, we will continue to use the existing Small School properties for educational courses during the evenings, weekends, and holidays.

After The Small School had been going for some years, people said, "Why don't you start something for adults?" That is how Schumacher College came about.

In 1990, when I was dreaming about establishing Schumacher College at Dartington in Devon, people said, "Your vision is too idealistic. Who is going to come to learn about ecology or spirituality or arts and crafts or holistic philosophy and pay for it?" Many thought that Schumacher College might last two or three years and then close. It is heartening and gratifying to see that after 28 years the college is still blossoming and flourishing.

The raison d'être behind Schumacher College was and still is very simple. Modern consumer society is promoted and supported by the mainstream educational system. The universities are the backbone of the military-industrial complex. Young people are conditioned to think in an economistic and materialistic way. The young people are taught to think that Nature is there for us to conquer and then use and exploit to maintain our high standard of living. We are educated to think that humans are the superior species and can do to Nature what we like. When students come out of universities, they often exploit Nature and other people in order to make their lives rich, comfortable, and successful. In this modern materialistic age, social injustice and ecological injustice merge.

We needed to challenge that. We could have done it in many ways. We could have spoken about it, written books about it. But that would not have been enough. We had to start something that showed another way, a better way, was possible. We do not have to condition young people's minds to exploit people or Nature. We need to teach that we *are* Nature. We need to live in harmony with Nature. Schumacher College was established to do just that. It is not only a place to teach ecology, but also a place where students can experience and live an ecological lifestyle.

In mainstream universities, the word *ecology* is defined very narrowly. It is the study of a particular organism in relation to its environment. At Schumacher College, we define it more broadly. The word *eco* means "home"—our planet home as well as our personal home. So not only is Schumacher College a place to learn ecology, in its broadest sense, but it is also a home in itself. That's the design of Schumacher College. We follow the Gandhian motto, "Be the change you want to see in the world." People who come to the college feel at home. They cook, they garden, they clean their rooms. If you go to a mainstream university, you have a blackboard on the wall, you have a computer screen on your desk, and there's a teacher by whom you are taught. Then you go back to your apartment or dormitory, and you live there. There is no connection between learning and living. Yet living and learning should be integral to each other. Theory and practice should merge with each other. This is the vision of holistic education. It is a process of learning by doing.

Schumacher College is a community as well as a home. We endeavor to live in harmony with Nature, with people, and with our surroundings. We learn to respect each other, help each other, and support each other. So we try to translate the idea of planet home and Earth community on a micro-level.

At the college, students learn holistic science, holistic economics, holistic philosophy, and how they are interrelated and interconnected. Ecology is connected with anthropology, anthropology is connected with psychology, and psychology is connected with gardening and agriculture. At the college, when you study a particular subject, you do so in the context of a bigger picture. Thus integrated learning and living is the essence of Schumacher College. Here students are transformed because they have gone through an experience of holistic living which included study, work, contemplation, and creative activities. Having transformed themselves, they go out into the world and find a way of transforming the world.

When these students leave the college, I urge them not to seek employment but to create their own work or livelihood, so many of our students have established their own businesses such as bookshops, whole food restaurants, wholefood shops, gardening, and writing. Some have gone to work for the United Nations in its climate change program, and others have set up environmental NGOs like the Carbon Disclosure Project. Some have joined environmental organizations such as Friends of the Earth or Greenpeace, or aid agencies such as Oxfam. One way or the other, many are working as agents of change. They help the world to be a better place, a place where everyone tries to minimize the exploitation of people and Nature and maximize spirituality, sustainability, and simplicity. Learning to live lightly, to live on less, and to make as small a footprint on the planet's resources as possible.

What characterizes learning at the college is that teachers and students work in partnership. Students do not consume knowledge; rather teachers and students explore and develop together. They are partners in learning. It's a journey. The students are there to discover themselves, their place on this planet Earth, and their purpose for being here. It's knowledge from the inside out, not from the outside in. Teachers are there to inspire, to ignite, to light the students' inner candle.

Nature is our teacher, as much as teachers like James Lovelock, Stephan Harding, Vandana Shiva, or any of our other visiting teachers. At least once a week, students go to Dartmoor, to the sea, or to the forest to learn and to experience Nature. In 28 years, thousands of students have come to the college. There are seventeen thousand on the alumni list. They learn, transform, and become agents of change. They enjoy and celebrate learning.

Schumacher College, named after the man who wrote *Small Is Beautiful*, needs to remain small. But more Schumacher College-type centers are emerging in other countries. They don't have to be called Schumacher College. It's not a franchise. People are using their initiative, based in the culture and ethos of their own country. Whatever the name, as long as these initiatives are holistic and people learn to serve their community, their society, and the Earth, then it is a Schumacher College. Such new centers of education are starting around the world and forming informal networks to support each other.

I often say to Schumacher students, "Go out into the world with confidence, don't look for a job but create your own job, create a livelihood. Live like an artist, like a karma yogi." There's a difference between having a job and having a livelihood. A job is something we do for money, whether we like it or not. Livelihood is where we do something we really want to do and find fulfillment in doing it. Being paid for it is a by-product. Of course we need money, but we are not working for money.

I want students to go out into the world and work for something greater—to work with imagination, work in the service of the Earth, and work for the values and ideals they hold dear in their hearts. They need to bring their profession and their vocation together. At the moment, many people have a vocation for their weekends, when they write poetry or paint or garden. They do something they enjoy doing, but during the weekdays, they toil in a profession. Their work is something they do to earn money. I want this separation of vocation and profession to be healed. Students must do what is their vocation *and* do it professionally. By combining the two, they transform their job into right livelihood.

At Schumacher College, 30 or 40 students of many different temperaments, nationalities, and religions live together. Over the years, they have come from Brazil and Japan, China and Chile, Mexico and Malaysia, from 90 countries in all. They learn to practice tolerance and acceptance, to be generous to each other, to celebrate different languages and cultures. They learn to speak with confidence and love. Words can wound or words can heal. So they learn the art of speaking and the art of listening. At the college, they learn to use loving speech which inspires trust. Students also learn the arts of cooking, cleaning, gardening, and other practical skills.

Our hands are a great gift. With our hands, we cook, we garden, and we write. Hands are our tools of transformation. The use of our hands deserves respect. At the moment, we are conditioned to think that working with our hands is somehow for the uneducated, for those who cannot write computer programs or do intellectual work. If you are a laborer or a gardener or a farm worker, your hourly rate might be about $10. But if you work in banking, in government, in business, or in a profession, you may get hundreds of dollars an hour. Thus our society has reduced the dignity and value of manual work. At Schumacher College, the dignity of doing things by hand is raised high.

At the college, we include cultivation of the heart. Caring for each other, developing empathy and compassion, is an integral part of learning. If we don't develop these qualities, our education will not be complete. We balance the education of head, heart, and hands. This is achieved by teachers setting an example and inspiring learners, showing them the importance of thinking, feeling, and making.

True learning occurs when the learner feels touched and moved by the experience, when what they learn is useful and helpful in their lives, when they acquire skills and techniques that enable them to express themselves and be part of their community.

Learning is not a race against time. It is a process of discovery which comes about when the learner is engaged and fully involved with her experience. For this to happen, there needs to be a relaxed atmosphere, where the learner doesn't feel any pressure, where he or she has the opportunity to learn at their own pace, and where the slow and simple activity of learning is celebrated. Learning is not about passing exams and getting good results. Learning is a process of self-realization.

We must remember that true learning does not take place only within the four walls of a school, a university, or a classroom. We learn all the time in life; formal education happens in addition to the ongoing learning taking place every moment. Somehow the importance of formal learning has been exaggerated. Jesus Christ didn't have a PhD in theology, nor did the Buddha acquire a master's degree in meditation. Formal education has a place, but we must keep it in its place, and not allow it to dominate our lives in such a way that if you have no formal education you are looked down upon.

The true art of learning is to cultivate curiosity. A learner's mind is a beginner's mind. We learn from the university of life and the university of Nature. The work of David Orr and Fritjof Capra—centered on the concept of ecoliteracy—provides an inspiring example of transformative learning. They argue that modern education does not equip people with true knowledge of life and Nature. So they have established the Ecoliteracy Institute in Berkeley, California. They point out that we live in an urban civilization. An increasing number of people have moved away from a natural and rural environment and live in cities, surrounded by cars and concrete buildings, cut off from the natural world. And therefore people are becoming eco-illiterate.

Ecoliteracy occurs when we are in Nature. It cannot be obtained from books or TV. There are wonderful Nature programs on television, but they cannot make us ecoliterate. For ecoliteracy, we have to experience Nature for ourselves.

If we wish to return to a proper relationship with the planet, we need to think of it as our home. *Eco* comes from the Greek *oikos*, which means "home." In the wisdom of Greek philosophers, *oikos* or *home* has many meanings. Home is where we live: our bedroom, bathroom, kitchen, and garden make our home. Then we have our village or city home, our regional home, and our national home. But ultimately we have to broaden our definition and deepen our understanding. We have to think about our planet home, our Earth home. Our primary home is the Earth itself. The word *logos* means "knowledge." So *ecology* or *ecoliteracy* means knowledge of home.

Home is also a place of relationships. Home is where we live with parents, brothers, sisters, husbands, wives, friends, and guests. Knowledge of home comes from understanding relationships.

Economy comes from the same root. *Nomos* means "management." So economy is management of home. We need to have knowledge of our home before we can manage it. A lot of people in universities study economy without studying ecology. This is why there is so much eco-illiteracy.

I was once invited to give a talk at the London School of Economics (LSE). I asked them, "Where is your department for ecology?" They said, "We haven't got one." I said,

"You are teaching your students economics, which means how to manage your home, without teaching them ecology, which means knowing what comprises a home? How are you going to manage your home if you don't know it?"

Ecology should come before economics, or at least ecology and economics should come together. It is like walking on two legs. If you walk only on one leg—the leg of economy—how long can you walk on it? After a little while, you will get tired. When you are tired, you fall down. No wonder that economies around the world are a story of crash after crash.

We have economic crises, environmental crises, global warming, population explosion, resource depletion. Why do we have these problems? Because we have been limping on one leg, the leg of economy. Now we need to sit down, relax, and prepare to walk on both legs. When we know our home, we will manage it better. We will know the limits of our home. We will learn to live simply and within our means. I suggested that they should change the name of their university and call it the LSEE, the London School of Ecology and Economics. But for them, this idea was too radical!

Economists and industrialists lack ecoliteracy. They do not seem to know the limits of the ecosystem. They go on to supervise the extraction of oil, minerals, and raw materials as if there were no tomorrow! If they were ecoliterate, if they knew our planet home, then they would know that these resources are finite. We cannot and should not make infinite demands upon raw materials that we extract from the finite Earth. Ecoliterate economists would know that there are natural laws under which our home, the Earth,

operates. One fundamental law of Nature which economists have ignored due to their lack of ecoliteracy is that all
natural systems are cyclical, whereas the modern economy
is linear. We extract natural resources, use them, and then
throw them away as waste. But in Nature, there is no waste.
Nature moves in cycles. The seasons move in cycles, the
Earth itself moves in a cycle, everything in Nature is cyclical.

From ecoliteracy we learn that everything moves in
cycles, and therefore everything must be recycled. There
should be no waste! Waste is a crime against Nature. Whatever natural material falls on the ground is absorbed by the
earth and turned into soil. In the autumn, leaves and fruit
fall and become part of the earth again, nutrition for the soil
and food for earthworms. The soil stores carbon within it.
Soil sequestrates, absorbs, and holds carbon to enrich life.
That carbon feeds the roots, the trunk, and the branches of
a tree. Then the sap rises again in the spring, and there are
blossoms and fruit once more.

Through this cyclical system, the leaves which fell onto
the ground reincarnate into new leaves. If you don't believe
in reincarnation, then you don't believe in the laws of Nature. Leaves on a tree die every year, and after death they
are resurrected again in the spring. Every year fresh leaves
are born. Life is eternal, spirit never dies. Through cyclical
systems, Nature always renews itself. The body of a tree is
recycled, the tree is born again as seed and the seed as a tree.
It is the law of Nature. Understanding this phenomenon is
part of ecoliteracy.

Unfortunately most graduates are eco-illiterate; this is
why, when they go out into the world of work, they not
only produce waste but create an economy which damages

the natural world, and causes many environmental problems. Many of these eco-illiterate economists working for governments, business, and industry are largely responsible for water pollution, air pollution, soil erosion, resource depletion, and climate change.

Knowledge by itself is dangerous. Highly educated scientists invented nuclear weapons and engage in genetic engineering. Uneducated peasant farmers don't produce nuclear weapons, nor do they produce genetically engineered seeds. Most of the problems of the world are caused by highly educated people who are paid hundreds of thousands of dollars for their work. As a result the Earth is now in peril. Therefore ecoliteracy is the imperative of our time.

Every student should take at least one day a week to be in Nature and sit by the bank of a river or sit under a tree, walk in the mountains, and learn from Nature. Nature herself is the greatest teacher. If university students want to be ecoliterate, they need to read the book of Nature. That is the greatest book, greater than the Bible, the Koran, or the Bhagavad Gita, greater than Shakespeare or Darwin. Great prophets and writers take inspiration from Nature. In *As You Like It*, Shakespeare speaks of "tongues in trees, books in the running brooks, sermons in stones and good in everything."

In "Inversnaid," Gerald Manley Hopkins wondered:

What would the world be, once bereft
of wet and of wilderness? Let them be left,
O let them be left, wilderness and wet;
Long live the weeds and the wilderness yet.

And Wordsworth wrote:

I wondered lonely as a cloud
That floats on high o'er vales and hills,
When all at once I saw a crowd,
A host, of golden daffodils;
Beside the lake, beneath the trees,
Fluttering and dancing in the breeze.

If there were no daffodils, there would be no Wordsworth. He was an ecoliterate poet par excellence.

All great art and literature comes from ecoliterate artists. Van Gogh sat in front of sunflowers and became an eco-artist. If there were no sunflowers, there would be no Van Gogh. People seldom value real sunflowers, they only think of Van Gogh in terms of the market value of his paintings that sell for 40 million dollars or more. They go to museums, but they have no time to sit in front of a living sunflower and contemplate Nature.

Monet created a garden so that he could paint water lilies, so that when he painted he could see Nature, closely, intimately, in detail. Monet observed the lilies hour by hour and day by day. Art and poetry are meditations on Nature.

Darwin studied earthworms, immersing himself in Nature, and from close observation of Nature developed the theory of evolution. He believed that we have come from Nature and we are Nature. Darwin's fundamental notion has been forgotten and often misinterpreted as "survival of the fittest." Nowadays in many universities, Nature has been reduced to an object of academic study. The old science tells us that Nature is red in tooth and claw. Scientists such as Francis Bacon advocated that we should manipulate and conquer Nature, and steal her secrets rather than trust her. Fortunately, the world of science is waking up, and new science sees unity between humans and Nature. Scientists such as James Lovelock and Lynne Margulis who have co-developed the science of Gaia believe that the Earth is a self-regulating benign system and it is our responsibility to learn to live in harmony with the Earth rather than exploit her.

In general, universities educate their students to be specialists; they have lost sight of the big picture. University graduates are half-educated. Being half-educated is worse than being uneducated. They are like half-baked bread. They have book knowledge but very little experience of Nature, which is the source of all life. Universities need a new pedagogy founded on the conviction that we need to learn about Nature and from Nature. We need to be humble, we need to create a Nature-centered education and an Earth-centered worldview.

We human beings are Nature. *Nature* in Latin means "birth." When a mother is about to give birth to a baby, she is given a prenatal check. *Natal* and *Nature* come from the same root. We humans are born, are we not? How can we say that Nature is only out there, or that trees, birds, bees, fruit, grass, rivers, and mountains are Nature but we humans are not?

First we separate ourselves from Nature, and then we think that humans are superior to Nature. We assume that Nature is there just for human benefit. A tree is there for its usefulness to humans. That tree is good because it will bring us $500 or it will give us fruit or oxygen. We value a tree only in terms of its usefulness to humans. That is human arrogance! Because of this arrogance, we think that we can do what we like to Nature. We can cut down rain forests, pollute rivers, overfish the oceans, and poison the land with agrochemicals because we are the superior species. We are the master species. Progressive groups have been trying to get rid of nationalism, sexism, and racism, but we are living under the spell of speciesism. We look at Nature as if she is our inferior, our servant. We've got rid of human slaves, but we treat Nature as our slave. Animals are treated as slaves too. We put animals in factory farms and inflict cruelties upon them. This is the result of our collective human ego, our egocentric worldview.

Now if we want to be ecoliterate, we have to shift from an egocentric to an ecocentric worldview. Ego views Nature as a possession; we say *my* land, *my* trees, *my* forest. I am the boss and I am in charge. This is the egocentric world-view. In the ecocentric worldview, there is no ownership *of* Nature, only relationship *to* Nature. We are all related, we are all connected, and the whole Earth is our home. We are members of this one Earth community and one Earth family. Birds flying in the sky, deer in the forest, butterflies on the bush, all creatures small and large are our brothers and sisters. They all have as much right to exist as humans have. Nature's rights are as important as human rights. In fact there is no need for human rights because Nature's rights include human rights since we are all Nature. Humans have rights to live and so have all other living beings.

Rather than human *rights*, we should talk about human *responsibility*. Nature has rights and humans have a responsibility not to destroy, pollute, or denigrate planet Earth. That is ecoliteracy.

In order to embrace ecoliteracy, we need to understand the deep meaning of education. There is a widely held view that a pupil or student is an empty vessel and the teacher's responsibility is to fill that vessel with as much factual information as possible. This is a mistaken understanding of education. The word *education* comes from the Latin word *educare*, which means "to lead out" or "to bring out" what is already there, to unfold what is dormant, to make explicit what is implicit.

Trees provide us with a good example. In Nature a seed becomes a tree, which then blossoms and gives fruit to humans and other living beings. Trees give oxygen to maintain life. In other words, trees serve the cause of sustaining life without any desire for self-aggrandizement. Particularly when trees are full of fruit, they bend low; they show humility and flexibility. When we are educated, we also need to serve the cause of life, enhance the Earth community, and sustain human relationships.

Trees mature by going through heat and cold, rain and drought. No tree has ever escaped stress. Only by suffering storms and hurricanes can trees become strong and resilient. If a tree is kept in the comfort of a greenhouse and protected from climatic conditions, it will not be so resilient and enduring. Trees have to be out in fields and forests to fend for themselves. The wilderness in which trees survive is the source of their strength.

In modern systems of organized and institutionalized education, we have lost a sense of the wild. People who grow up in indigenous cultures know the art of living. They use their hands and legs as well as their heads and hearts. They know how to connect, how to relate, how to appreciate, how to celebrate, and how to endure. They are self-reliant. Modern education creates humans who lack the skills and confidence to be resilient and self-reliant and to serve selflessly. Modern education creates job seekers and employees, and many jobs consist of minding machines or shifting papers. Even farmers hardly touch the soil or seeds, they no longer harvest crops or milk cows with their hands. They mostly drive huge tractors and combine harvesters. Increasingly farms are worked not by farmers but by robots.

Humans are no longer masters of their machines; machines have become the masters of humans. Machines have replaced human hands, and in the robotic age, we face the prospect of robots replacing humans altogether. Modern education is not only responsible for deskilling but also for dehumanizing humans.

In order for us to integrate facts with feelings and to shift from information to knowledge, we need to introduce the idea of learning by doing—of using our heads, our hearts, and our hands. Wisdom arises when knowledge and experience meet. The task of education is not to produce ever-increasing numbers of consumers but to help humans become makers and creators, using their intuition and imagination as well as skill and technique.

We need to offer all people opportunities to learn craft skills, such as pottery, woodwork, weaving, mending, and repairing. The status of making and crafting should be equal to the status of science, maths, and literature. This is the way of learning by doing which is exemplified by The Small School, Schumacher College, and the Center for Eco-literacy.

It is time to recover the original meaning of education, education as a process of self-discovery. During this educational adventure, we need to embrace uncertainties, ambiguities, difficulties, and hardships. This means being prepared to face problems rather than running away from them. Only when we face problems can we use our imagination to solve them. In the comfort of the classroom, we can obtain information; in the luxury of libraries, we can gain knowledge, but experience can be gained only when we are out in the storm of life and in the rough terrain of Nature.

If we wish to live simply, meaningfully, creatively, and imaginatively, then we have to follow a system of education which frees us from the idea of self-centered individualism, from the notion of separation from "the other," and from the concept of a disconnected "self." Training in elegant simplicity has to be rooted in the soil of right relationships. I will address this theme in the next chapter.

The easy way is also the right way.

— Bruce Lee

right relationships:
we are all related

Relationships
based on
obligation
lack dignity.
Wayne Dwyer

ELEGANT SIMPLICITY can only be built on the firm foundation of right relationships. Our crises—mental, personal, social, economic, environmental, political, cultural, and religious—have their origin in disconnection and separation. The moment we see that all things are connected, that we are all related, that everything depends on everything else, we start to see solutions. Why do we have crises between Palestine and Israel, between Sunni and Shia, between America and Russia, India and Pakistan, Christians and Muslims? Because we see ourselves as being separate from others. When all our interactions are embedded in friendships and loving relationships, then we will act from a position of patience, acceptance, tolerance, forgiveness, and generosity.

When I was 27, I spent two and a half years walking around the world, which I have described in Chapter Two. I walked for eight thousand miles, without any money, completely depending on the hospitality of people. I was able to do this because in my mind there was no separation. All beings were my family and friends. The whole Earth was my home.

When my friend Menon and I crossed the border from India to Pakistan, I said, "If we go as Indians, we will meet Pakistanis, Russians, or Americans. If we go as Hindus, we will meet Muslims, Christians, Buddhists, or Jews. If we go as Gandhians, we'll meet capitalists, communists, or socialists. These are all labels which divide us. I don't want to go as an Indian, a Hindu, a Gandhian. I want to go simply as a human being, then wherever I go I will meet human beings. I'll be able to make friends with all of them."

Our true identity is that we are members of one human community, and moreover we are part of one Earth community. Trees are our kith and kin, birds flying in the sky, bees and wasps, butterflies and snakes, tigers and elephants are all our kith and kin.

We need to understand that all species are related to each other, all of us have evolved together. The sun heats the soil, the soil feeds the trees, the trees feed the birds, the rain feeds the trees. All beings nourish each other. This is ecology.

This system cannot be measured or quantified. People talk about ecosystems services. They want to put a monetary value on natural resources. But I say, "Tell me how much value I should put on the air I have just inhaled?" This little breath—how much value can you put on it? Can ecosystems services value this air that I am breathing? No one can put value on the air we breathe. Can we say, "My mother feeds me with her milk. How much does that cost? Five dollars? Ten dollars?" You cannot put a price on mother's milk. When we have this understanding, then we will value relationships more than monetary measures.

The appropriate way to manage the economy is to have right relationships with all species in our Earth home. At present, people don't understand the true meaning of economics. When the Chancellor of the Exchequer or a finance minister talk about the economy, they actually mean finance, banks, and money. But money is not the economy.

We should call this "moneynomics." True economics is land, labor, and capital. These three are the foundation of the economy. Land represents the entire natural world. Everything comes from the land, and everything goes back to the land. Wise management of the land—of trees, rivers, mountains, forests, soil, animals, and fishes—is the basis of the real economy. But the government says, "Looking after the environment gets in the way of the economy." In fact, there cannot be any economy without the environment. That's why land is the first principle of the economy. The economy is a wholly owned subsidiary of the environment. Therefore our right relationship with the environment is the foundation of a good economy.

The second strand to the economy is labor, which means people, their imagination, creativity, and skills. People are the real wealth. It is they who create and maintain the economy. Therefore right relationships with and between people are essential for a thriving economy.

The third strand is financial capital. Money is a measure of wealth. It is like a map which is useful to find the territory; but a map is not the territory. Money is a map of wealth, not wealth itself. One million pounds could be the cost of building a house. But the money is not the house, and the house is not the money. We cannot live in money, we can only live in a house.

Thus financial capital and money have a place in the economy, as a form of exchange and facilitating transactions, but we must keep them in their place, and not allow them to dominate our entire economic system. The money economy has transformed land and labor into commodities, and making money has become the sole purpose of modern economies. As a result, land and labor are the victims of diminishing value. What we need is a system which values these three at an appropriate level in the context of an integrated whole.

These three aspects of the economy belong to each other. In our body we have a brain to think, a heart to feel, eyes to see, a nose to smell, a tongue to eat, ears to hear. We don't have any separation. All our organs and faculties are interconnected parts of one body. The human body is a microcosm of the macrocosm. The entire universe is in our body, we are stardust, we are made of the sun, the moon, earth, air, fire, water, consciousness, space, time, imagination, and creativity, all of this in one body and in constant interaction. But in the field of economics, we have separated finance from ethics, and the environment from people. This disconnection is the biggest problem of our times. "Only connect" is the solution. We need to reconnect everything. When we are connected in right relationship with all human beings and also with the more-than-human world, then we will be in harmony with ourselves and with the entire ecosystem in its multiplicity and diversity.

Diversity is essential for right relationships. Therefore diversity is something to be celebrated. Diversity should not be turned into division. Division is to say, you are on the left, I am on the right, and then to consider one side as superior to the other. A left wing and a right wing belong to the same bird. Why do we think we should cut off the right wing or the left wing? We need a left hand and a right hand, both are of equal value. When left and right are in right relationship, then there is completeness and wholeness. Then all crises are transformed into opportunities.

The house of right relationship is built on the foundation of friendship. Friendship is the best and purest form of relationship. Personally speaking, all my work has emerged out of friendships; *Resurgence & Ecologist* magazine, which I edited for over 40 years, is a result of friendship. I have so many good friends who have contributed articles, artwork, and money to the magazine. The Small School and Schumacher College grew out of friendship.

Friendship is the primary principle and the bread and butter of my life. Take my food away, but not friendship! I live by friendship. It is supremely spiritual. Friendship is unconditional—there are no "ifs" and no "buts." There is no reason why somebody is a friend. I don't say, "I am your friend because you are educated, or rich, or intelligent, or handsome, or you are good to talk to." Such things don't come to my mind. I am a friend and I have a friend because I want to be a friend. Friendship is all about acceptance, without expectations. We give and we receive. Friendship is rooted in deep gratitude.

In friendship you only say yes. There is only yes. If somebody asks me for some help out of friendship, I always say yes. And if I ask someone out of friendship, in my experience they too always say yes.

My friendship is not only for humans. I feel friendship towards Nature too. I am a friend of my home and my garden. I am a friend of trees and flowers. I am a friend of the bees. I am a friend of earthworms, slugs, and snails. Weeds are my friends. Friendship is a term people use mostly for human relationships, but I use it in a broader sense.

My children are my friends. In India we say that when your children become 16 they are no longer your children;

they are your friends. "Friend" is a better term than "son" or "daughter" because son and daughter carry expectations. You expect something from your children. They expect something from you as parents. As friends you don't expect anything. You treat them in a respectful way. It is the same with my wife. She is my friend. My relationship with her is not possessive. Love liberates. There is no bondage and there is no attachment in such a marriage. Again it is a relationship rooted in acceptance and freedom from expectations.

The village where I live is my friend. I accept it as it is. I don't sit in judgment. I love my village. I love its people, its valleys, and trees. I love the landscape. I live near the Atlantic Ocean. The ocean is my friend. The whole Earth is my friend. The whole world is my friend. Whatever transformation I am trying to bring in my life, in my society, and in the world, I do with a sense of friendship.

My home is my friend. Because after a while my home needs renewal, I clean it, I repair it, and I paint it. And my garden sometimes needs renewal. So I weed, put compost on the soil, or even let the land lie fallow for a year. When my body needs renewing and healing, I slow down and have a siesta. The world is beautiful, but society's politics and economics need renewal too. So I work to bring renewal there as well. I participate in the process of transformation. I say to society, "Have a siesta, slow down, don't work too fast or too hard." It is all out of friendship. The Buddha said: "Too fast or too forceful, you miss the way."

My work at The Small School was an act of friendship for children. My work for *Resurgence & Ecologist* magazine is in the service of my readers. At Schumacher College, I act to promote ecology and spirituality in the world. My work is that of a friendly healer.

So it's out of friendship that I would advise the leaders in Europe: "Look at Mr. Putin and see him as a friend, then your conflicts will dissolve." I would say to Mr. Putin: "Treat all Ukrainians as your friends. You are a Christian. What did Jesus say? 'Love your neighbor!'" I would say to Mr. Netanyahu: "You have been at war with the Palestinians for the past 70 years. What have you achieved? Try friendship with Palestine for once, and see what happens. Through friendship all pains are healed." I would advise the Palestinians: "The Jews have been in exile for two thousand years. Now they have to come home. Welcome them. Together you can turn Palestine into a land of milk and honey." The best way to have a friend is to be a friend. Friendship is the easy and simple answer to all our agonies, anxieties, and anguish, to all our disputes, conflicts, and wars.

In friendship there are no expectations. Things never work out as we expect, so expectations often bring disappointment. I practice acceptance. I am detached and keep moving; I am not stuck and there is no bondage. Detachment brings freedom. When I work for transformation in the world out of friendship, then I work for my own transformation as I am my own friend. In the cosmic sense of friendship, I expand my consciousness, I see my greater self, the universal self. In this body, I am the microcosm of the macrocosm. The is the deep Buddhist meaning of friendship which goes beyond everyday acquaintances.

In the field of friendship, we sow the seeds of love with the hands of humility. We spread the compost of kindness and irrigate the soil of our souls with the water of generosity. We need to give thanks, with deep gratitude, for all the gifts of life that we receive every day. Then we are blessed with the fruits of freedom. It is sweet to be a friend, and it is a blessing to have friends.

Whether we are Russians or Americans, Jews or Arabs, Shia or Sunni, communists or capitalists, whatever the label, we are human beings first and foremost. Our primary human identity supersedes all other secondary identities. That is why we have to build our personal, political, economic, and ecological relationships on the foundation of friendship.

Friendship is the only glue to hold humanity together. Through the philosophy of friendship, we realize that we are all connected, we are all related, we are all interdependent.

When the Buddha was breathing his last breath, Ananda asked him, "How would you like to be reincarnated in your next life?" The Buddha answered: "Not as a prophet, not as a teacher, but simply as *maitreya*. I wish to be reincarnated as a friend." Wherever there is the presence of friendship, there is the presence of god. God comes to us in the form of a friend.

You might call me an idealist. Yes, I am an idealist. But I ask you, "What have the realists achieved? Wars? Poverty? Climate change?" The realists have ruled the world for far too long and have failed to achieve peace and prosperity for all. So let us give the idealists a chance, and let friendship be the organizing principle of our life and our world. We may not be one hundred percent successful. We may not achieve utopia, but let us maximize the power of friendship and minimize the force of conflicts. Let us have no enemies, make no enemies, and be no enemy. This is worth trying.

There is no better way to establish right relationship than through friendship, so give no offense and take no offense.

Animosity, conflict, quarrels, anger, isolation, and loneliness make life much too complicated and confused. Right relationship, based in the purity of friendship, makes life simple and straightforward. But the ideal of friendship is more than polite manners or superficial social gestures or expedient diplomatic etiquette. Relationship is not an obligation, it is the very ground of our existence. Relationship and friendship have to be the fruit of all authentic and radical love. So how does love bring us to simplicity, and how does simplicity bring us back to love?

Elegance is achieved when all that is superfluous has been discarded. The simpler the posture the more beautiful it will be.

— PAUL COELHO

love unlimited

There is no charm equal
to tenderness of heart.

Jane Austen

THE PUREST AND DEEPEST expression of elegant simplicity comes with the experience of love. Love is like the wind; we don't see it but we feel it.

To love is to accept the other as the other is, without judgment. By the same token, love is to accept myself for who I am. On the basis of acceptance, we participate in the process of evolution, transformation, and change. Love is to go with the flow of life and grow in the glow of gracious mutuality.

First of all we need to fall in love with ourselves. Often we want to fall in love with someone else without loving ourselves. Yet it is only when we fall in love with ourselves that we are ready to fall in love with someone else. Self-acceptance prepares us for accepting others. We need to accept ourselves unconditionally in order to accept someone else unconditionally.

When we go to a party, we prepare ourselves. We wash our face, brush our hair, we dress, put on good shoes. Then we go to the party. In the same way, when we want to fall in love with somebody, we need to pay attention to ourselves. I am going to fall in love because I am happy, relaxed, and free.

Christ said, "Love your neighbor as yourself." The word *yourself* is the key term. As you love yourself, love others. The implication is that if you don't love others that is because you don't love yourself. The other is only an extension of yourself. Loving your self is not selfish! If you cannot love yourself, how can you love someone else, and why should you expect someone else to love you?

Accepting yourself as you are and loving yourself for being who you are is a prerequisite for loving others as they are and for being who they are. This is the reality of interbeing. We are all interdependent. We are made of each other. Therefore loving yourself does not mean being separated and isolated from others.

Self-love has nothing to do with pride, arrogance, or ego. It is the ego that builds the walls of separation. It is the ego that wants name, fame, and recognition. Craving prestige, power, and domination is the work of the ego.

As the soil is the source of all fruits, flowers, and foods, so the soul is the ground of the intellect and the imagination, of love and compassion. And as the soil is the source of weeds, thorns, and all things rough and rugged, harsh and craggy, the soul is the ground of anxiety, anguish, and agony. We need to accept them and transform them with love. Love of yourself, love of your neighbor, love of people, and love of Nature are a continuum. We need to be kind to ourselves and to all others so that no one needs to be subjected to suffering. This is radical love.

In radical love it is not that I want to *have* a lover but rather that I want to *be* a lover. When I say "I love you," I have made an unconditional offer of love. Whether the other person loves me or not is not in my control.

How do I love someone? Should I love on my terms or on the terms of the person I love? If it is true love, then I would not say, "I will love you if you are like this or like that." The moment I put conditions on my love, I miss the point of true love. Falling in love is to surrender ego, to say, "I love you as you are, whoever you are," imposing no conditions, no expectations. That's pure love, true love on all levels—physical, emotional, and spiritual. Desireless love. Desireless love is not unromantic. Romantic love includes sexual love, but goes beyond it. It is love with the whole being, body and soul.

Romantic poets like Wordsworth fell in love with Nature. Other romantic painters like Turner fell in love with the landscape. Shelley and Keats fell in love with life. Romance is an integral part of love. We need to fall in love as Wordsworth fell in love with flowers. Falling in love is not a once-in-a-lifetime experience. We can fall in love every day as Turner fell in love with the sea every day. A lover says to the beloved, "My darling, how beautiful you are, how wonderful you are. You are magic. You are still with me in spite of my shortcomings, my faults, and my dreadful behavior. I am blessed. I love you."

In our rational age, we are told that being a romantic is not good. This is mistaken. We have to restore the place of romance in our lives. Love is not a matter of pragmatism. Love is not a marriage of convenience. Love is a union of body and soul. A loving relationship is a most precious thing. Two people come together with different temperaments and cultures. Accepting these differences is not easy. When two people come together, they do not merge with each other. Falling in love is not a merger. We come together to stand side by side. One plus one is not two, it is eleven: $1 + 1 = 11$. When we are in a loving relationship we say, "I am your support. I am here for you. Lean on me."

Because of our upbringing and conditioning, we may be used to doing things in a certain way. When we start to accept and appreciate somebody else's way of doing things and not expect the other person to do things our way, then we begin to lay the foundation for a truly loving and resilient relationship. In close relationships, it's the small things that really matter. Small disagreements can create big conflicts. A big beautiful book is made up of small beautiful sentences. A great relationship of love is made of small acts of kindness.

The universe would not exist without sexual love. When man and woman come together, embrace each other, kiss each other, and make love, then a child is conceived. Each and every one of us are products of romantic love. We should celebrate sexual love without being shy about it. We can praise it, sing about it, and write poems about it. Giving our body to somebody else and receiving somebody else's body into ours is a beautiful act. Humans, animals, plants, bees, and flowers all come together in such an intimate union. The design of the universe is based on the biology of love. Without male and female, *shiva* and *shakti*, yin and yang coming together, life cannot exist. The universe is union in love. Love is the source of procreation and pleasure.

Each of our senses has a dual purpose. One is to enable us to live. The other is to give us pleasure. For example, food is like fuel for the body. We could have vitamin pills and protein pills and survive. But mere survival is not enough. The universal design is to make food tasty, fragrant, and colorful so that it is not just sustenance for the body, it is also a source of joy. We say, "Delicious food, strawberries, apples, baked potatoes, rice, wow!" We look at flowers and feel pleasure. We hear music and poetry, and they give us pleasure. Our body is made for pleasure as well as for all its functions. It absorbs joy like blotting paper.

Similarly, sex is for procreation and reproduction, but the design of the universe is such that while we are making a baby, we are also expressing our love for each other, giving as well as receiving pleasure, joy, and delight. We have function and pleasure at the same time. We engage in relationships of love with a sense of the sacred, of beauty, of respect, of reverence, and surrender of the ego. There resides joy. Sex without love is like a flower without fragrance or a well without water.

In India sex is sacred. When we go into a Shiva temple what do we find? Not an altar, not a statue, not a picture, but a phallus in union with the female organ. The male and female organs in union are worshipped. They are *Shiva* and *Shakti*. The West has romantic poetry and romantic painting, the East has a romantic religion.

In the temple of Khajuraho in central India, we can see statues depicting 84 postures of sexual union, explicitly portrayed. This is a temple, not a museum, not an art gallery, not a night club, but a temple. People go there to worship gods and goddesses making love.

No Indian god exists without the goddess. Shiva is with Shakti, Rama with Sita, Krishna with Radha and many other lovers, called gopis.

When we refer to Hindu gods, the female name comes before the male. We say, Sita Rama, not Rama Sita. Sita is female and Rama is male. Lakshmi Narayan not Narayan Lakshmi. Lakshmi is the female and Narayan is the male.

Radha Krishna. Radha is the female, Krishna the male. So the woman is first because it is the woman who brings the world into existence. It is the mother principle which is supreme. At the Sri Aurobindo ashram in Auroville, the temple is not of Sri Aurobindo but of the mother; *matrimandir*, the temple of the mother. Ultimately it is in the union of male and female that the god of love resides. God in India is a god of love, and religion is a religion of love. It is as simple as that!

In the male-female union, Hindus practise tantric sex. They stay in the state of orgasm as long as possible. They believe that the orgasmic state is the highest state of transcendence, a complete surrender of ego. Everything is suspended. In the state of orgasm, the personal beloved is in a state of union with the divine beloved. The lovers are in state of total ecstasy and equilibrium. The mind is completely free of duality and divisions.

When we are truly in love, we are in love all the time. We are in love every moment. The moment we wake up, we fall in love with the beautiful sky and sunrise, we fall in love with flowers and butterflies. We see god in a grain of sand and the divine beloved in a blade of grass. We fall in love with a woman, a man, with parents, with children, with everyone. It's love for the sake of love. There is no other motivation. I worship no other god but the god of love.

Love is the means and also the end. Love is the way and also the destination. There is no way to love, love is the way. Love is a way of being. We have to learn to love what we do and do only what we love. As Confucius said, "If you choose to do what you love then you will never have to work, even for a day in your life."

Love is unlimited and unconditional. It has no such thought as "I will love you *if* you love me," or "I will love you *but* you have to be good." True love is to love even when someone is less than perfect. Because it is love which makes everyone perfect. It is easy to love someone who loves you and who is good. But true unconditional love is to love even when you don't receive love in return. Love is not for the fainthearted. It requires courage and conviction. Love grows in the ground of grace and gratitude.

Our world is not sustained by anger, pride, hatred, aggression, or war. These negative forces are the shadow side of our nature. Ultimately we are sustained by love. Generosity, kindness, and trust are different aspects of love. The essence of life is love.

In our personal life, how often do we get angry? Once a day? Once every other day? Once a week? When we do get angry, how long does it last? Five minutes? Five hours? Five days? Anger and hatred are occasional and short-lived. For it is love that endures. Love is forever.

There are about seven billion people in the world. How many people at any one time are engaged in wars and aggressive acts? Five million? Ten million? Always a minority. The majority of people live in love and peace with each other, helping and caring for each other.

Dictators and tyrants are not our heroes. The Buddha and Jesus Christ are followed by millions because they walked the path of love. The world admires Mahatma Gandhi, Nelson Mandela, Mother Teresa, and Martin Luther King because they preached and practiced the politics of love. Who wants to follow in the footsteps of Hitler or

Stalin? Even when some armed revolutionaries are praised, it is not for their violence that they are admired, but for their struggle for justice and their love of ordinary people. Governments have put their faith in the force of arms, but people in general live by the power of love and they are happier for that. Love is the ideal and love is also practical politics. In love there is true security.

Love is to accept bitter with the sweet, gain with loss, pain with pleasure, all with equanimity. The moment we bring love into play, through our imagination we transform the illusion of separateness into a unity between all; thus duality becomes unity. We transcend likes and dislikes and enter into the celebration of life as it is. When we drink the sweet nectar of love, a miracle occurs. There is transformation. As Jalal ad-Din Rumi, the Sufi poet, said:

> By love, the bitter becomes sweet
> By love, copper coins become gold
> By love, the dregs become clear
> By love, the pain becomes healing...

This is the transformative power of love.

Life is a landscape of love, and love is the celebration of life. Love is not logic, love is pure magic. Love is pure poetry and pure pleasure.

Allow yourself to be swept away by the force of love. To love is to be free from criticizing, complaining, and comparing. To practice universal love is to recognize that those who behave badly do so because they have not been loved. W.H. Auden goes even further when he says, "Those to whom evil is done / Do evil in return."

And William Blake tells us:

Love to faults is always blind,
Always is to joy inclin'd,
Lawless, wing'd and unconfin'd,
And breaks all chains from every mind.

When Christ said "love your enemy," he did not say it lightly. He was serious. He believed that "amor vincit omnia," love conquers all. By love, enemy becomes friend. Love keeps no record of wrongdoings. Love requires courage to turn the other cheek. To love is to be brave. Sing the song of love and all your worries and miseries will evaporate! Live in the ecstasy of love. Then you will be sustained by love.

To love is to see god, because god is love and love is god. To mystics and Sufi poets, god appears as the beloved and the beloved as god. Love is the greatest religion on Earth. Love is the mother of all virtues—peace and compassion, generosity and humility are born from love. Love is majestic and magnificent. Where there is love, there is hope. Love and rejoice.

Lovers take no offense and give none. Lovers take no enemies, make no enemies, and have no enemies. Animosity is a consequence of hate, and friendship is the consequence of love. As bees love flowers and produce honey, lovers love each other and produce happiness. Love is the purpose of life, and through love we find the meaning of life.

To live is to love and to love is to risk, to risk being hurt, to risk the possibility of not being loved in return. Do not wish to have a lover, simply be a lover. Having a lover is a result of being a lover.

Love awakens the soul, love nourishes the heart, love brings joy to our lives. Love is the most beautiful mantra of the mind. The balm of love heals all wounds, the wounds of anger and anxiety, the wounds of fear and resentment.

Love of yourself, love of your beloved, love of people, and love of Nature are a continuum. We need to be kind to ourselves and to all others so that no one needs to be subjected to suffering and everyone can experience the joy of love and drink its nectar.

Love is as natural to us as breathing. Rumi says, "Your task is not to seek for love but merely to seek and find all the barriers within yourself that you have built against it."

This all-embracing love manifests through many forms, such as philology (love of learning), philosophy (love of wisdom), and philanthropy (love of people). More intimately we experience erotic love. How beautiful it is to fall in love and be in the embrace of one's beloved! But falling in love is not an event taking place only once in a lifetime. If we want, we can and we should fall in love every day. Falling in love is a miracle. We are born thanks to the act of making love. Everyone is a love child. There is no original sin, only original love.

Love takes us beyond reason, beyond intellect, and beyond description. Love brings us to a place beyond right and wrong, a place of magnanimity and generosity. This is deep love of life. All we need is love because love is everything. Love is the answer. What is your question?

However, we are human, and from time to time, we fall from the grace of love into the disgrace of hate, anger, and resentment. Just as our normal state is a state of health but from time to time we fall ill, and we need remedies to heal our sickness. Similarly, when we are overcome with the sickness of hate, we need the remedy of forgiveness. Forgiveness is the antidote to hate, fear, and anger. Hate, fear, and anger can occupy our emotions, our minds, and our souls. With the broom of forgiveness, we can sweep this dust from our minds and restore the simplicity of love. I will dwell in the house of forgiveness in the next chapter.

When I know enough is enough
I already have enough.
When I don't know when enough is enough
I will never have enough.

— INDIAN PROVERB

power of forgiveness

It's one of
the greatest
gifts you can
give yourself,
to forgive.
Forgive
everybody.

Maya Angelou

To live simply and practice spiritual simplicity, I had to acquire the power of forgiveness. During my eight-thousand-mile walk across the continents, I faced a gun twice. Once in Paris and a second time in Atlanta, Georgia, in the United States. In Paris I was mistaken by a white Frenchman with a gun for an Algerian terrorist. This was at the time when the Algerian war was coming to an end, and he thought I might be dangerous. It was ironic. I had just walked all the way from India to Paris via Moscow, promoting peace, nonviolence, and forgiveness, and here I was in the heart of civilization being misidentified as someone violent, maybe a terrorist.

I escaped death thanks to a friend whom I was visiting. She explained to the gunman that I was no terrorist, I was her friend, I was a peacemaker. Afterwards she wanted to report my assailant to the police, but I said, "The man who was carrying the gun is full of fear. He is afraid of losing something, perhaps his superiority as a white man, perhaps his life itself, or some other fear. In the end he has to come to terms with his fear and overcome it. This cannot be done by locking him up."

My host said, "But you might have been killed!"

I replied, "Yes, I might have, but one can only die once. One can live a long life full of fear and revenge. I do not wish to live like that."

The second story is similar. In 1964 after meeting Martin

Luther King in Atlanta, Georgia, an English friend invited me to a restaurant not knowing that it was for whites only. The waiters refused to serve us so I went up to see the manager to ask for an explanation. He said, "We don't do explanations, leave immediately, no ifs, no buts."

I replied "No I am not leaving." By now I realized that the cause for the refusal was the color of my skin.

"Get out!" he shouted at me. Waiters and customers gathered around.

I said, "I am sorry, but why are you angry? I have done no harm to you. I am only asking for a cup of tea. We can pay for it in advance. Is there any problem?"

The manager opened a drawer, pulled out a gun, and said, "Get out immediately or…" By now many more people had gathered, and they and the waiters took hold of me and pushed me out the door.

Later I complained about the incident to the State Department because I thought the US government needs to know what is going on in the restaurants of their country. My intention was not to seek punishment for the restaurateur but, hopefully, to change the law. I received an apology from the State Department. But in any case, I felt no bitterness. The proprietor was acting out of fear, the fear of losing white superiority, the fear of being overwhelmed by the power of the black minority. Martin Luther King stated that the white community did not need to fear the black. The black community did not wish to rule over the white, but neither did they wish to be ruled by them. We are all equal in the eyes of God. Whatever color we are, we all have red blood under our skin. Basic human dignity and the dignity of life is the prerogative of us all.

I have learned that the art of forgiveness can go hand in hand with the art of acting for a just cause. Forgiveness does not mean surrender to injustice, and acting for justice does not mean taking revenge or inflicting injury upon your opponent.

For me, the practice of forgiveness goes back to my Jain roots. As a child monk until the age of 18, every night before going to bed I would chant a mantra of forgiveness:

> I forgive all living beings upon this earth.
> I beg forgiveness from all living beings.
> I cherish friendship with all living beings.
> I have no enemies.

If I lay down having forgotten to say this prayer, I would get up, close my eyes, be still, and chant the mantra twice. It was not just a case of uttering the words. I would feel the meaning deeply, along with a profound sense of my unity with all life. "The idea that anyone can be your enemy is false," said my guru. "You make an enemy of the other only through your fear, so your fear is your enemy. Conquer fear and you have conquered all enemies."

In addition to this daily practice, Jains have an annual festival of forgiveness. During the monsoon season, there is a day when all Jains fast for 24 hours. I consumed nothing but boiled water and spent all my waking hours remembering thoughts, words, or actions which may have been harsh or harmful and which may have caused hurt to someone during the year. This was a time of sincere and genuine reflection. I repeated the words "I forgive, I forgive, I forgive" after each recollection of anger, irritation, or arrogance. As I sought forgiveness from others, I also forgave myself for my shortcomings.

I remember vividly that after 24 hours of physical and mental detoxification, I felt light and healed, as if a huge burden had been taken from my shoulders. After breaking my fast, I went to my friends and family members and asked for forgiveness face to face. I bowed down and touched the feet of my fellow monks and told them in all sincerity that I harbored no ill feeling or sense of hurt even if they had annoyed me. I came to seek forgiveness and also to give forgiveness.

On this day, Jains also write letters asking for forgiveness and giving forgiveness if their friends and family are not near enough for them to do so in person. Forgiving yourself, forgiving your fellow human beings, and seeking forgiveness from others creates the ground on which compassion, generosity, mutuality, reciprocity, communication, and love can grow. There cannot be a sense of harmony and peace without forgiveness.

Freedom from fear is the fruit of forgiveness. When we are free from fear, we can create conditions conducive to the creativity which is absolutely necessary for human well-being. When we are boiling with rage and the desire for revenge, we are incapable of finding physical, mental, or spiritual fulfillment. Happiness is a consequence of a calm mind. According to Jains, the purpose of life is to find happiness or *ananda*. Happiness occurs when we make no enemies, when we have no enemies, when we give no offense and take no offense. If someone tries to be an enemy, we can often dissolve their animosity through patience and forgiveness.

Forgiveness is only possible when someone has hurt us, wounded us, or insulted us. Such negative acts offer us an opportunity to cultivate and manifest compassion which is the antidote to revenge. If no one acted negatively or harmfully, then there would be no opportunity to practice forgiveness. If someone hurts us and we hurt them back, then we descend to their level. Their violence plus our violence doubles the amount of violence. An increase of aggression helps no one. One cannot extinguish a fire by putting on more fuel. The only way to put out the fire of aggression and anger is with the water of forgiveness. The water of forgiveness is not merely a passive process of not reacting negatively. The water of forgiveness is a positive action to see good in an individual even when you are faced with extreme negativity.

Vinoba Bhave used to explain the royal road to forgiveness to us. There are some skeptics who can only see faults in everyone. Their skepticism prevents them from practicing forgiveness. Then there are people who see some good and some bad in everyone; these are the rationalists. For them, practicing forgiveness is also difficult. Then there are people who mainly see good in everyone. They can begin to practice forgiveness. Then there are those who, on finding some small virtue in others, magnify it, praise it extravagantly, and shower them with appreciation. These are the people on the royal road to forgiveness.

I questioned whether this kind of behavior was honest and truthful. Vinoba responded that when you see a small virtue in someone, you need to realize that this good quality represents a reservoir of virtue hidden in their hearts. By focusing on that virtue, you shine a light on it. It is comparable to reading a map in which one inch represents ten miles. Although on the map you see an inch, you know that on the ground it is ten miles. In the same way, you may look at one small virtue in a badly behaved person and know that he or she has the potential to be a saint. In fact, it is possible to transform an evil person into a saint by forgiveness.

Vinoba himself had great generosity of spirit. No wonder he was able to inspire and persuade landlords, often thought to be mean and greedy, to donate land and share their wealth with the landless poor. It was a miracle that Vinoba collected 4.5 million acres of land in gifts which were distributed among the lowest of the low, laborers who possessed nothing. At public meetings, in Vinoba's presence, landlords asked for forgiveness from the poor who their families had exploited for generations. In return the landless laborers offered forgiveness to the landlords under whose regime they and their ancestors had suffered. The exchange of forgiveness healed the wounds of lifetimes. At last, in many villages there was reconciliation and peace.

Another example in Vinoba's life was the surrender of bandits and dacoits (armed robbers) who were ravaging and pillaging the rural population of central India. This came about because Vinoba dared to go to them with love and the force of forgiveness. He spoke to them with respect. "You are rebels, I too am a rebel, the only difference between us is that I use the weapon of compassion. But I praise you for your spirit of rebellion and courage, let us join together to bring justice and equality to our society." Until then everybody had condemned these people and called them criminals, but Vinoba called them rebels, men of courage. His words brought about a change of heart, and these armed rebels surrendered their weapons, seeking and giving forgiveness. They had to undergo the legal process and received a period of imprisonment, but they gained a new respect and praise from the public, the press, and the government. Eventually they and their families were rehabilitated by being given land to farm and capital to start cottage industries.

Although as a young monk I had been taught the annual ritual of forgiveness, as an adult I learned that the practice of forgiveness is not always easy. In some cases, it may take many years to arrive at a state of complete forgiveness. I had to struggle that long to forgive my mother and my guru.

My mother was flexible and tolerant in most aspects of her life, but when it came to religious principles, she was strict, almost rigid. When I left the monastic order and went home expecting a warm welcome from my beloved mother, I was totally taken aback when she said, "No, you cannot come home." She did not even offer me a glass of water.

"But I am your son," I begged.

"No, you are not. You renounced home nine years ago, you committed yourself to being a monk for life, so go back to Gurudev, ask his forgiveness, and beg to be readmitted to the order."

I could not believe my ears. Was this the same mother who loved me so much? I was deeply disappointed, upset, and angry.

"I am not going back to the monks," I said, "and you are never going to see me again." With this threat, I turned my back on her, and found my way to a Gandhian ashram in Bodh Gaya.

Many years later, my mother and my guru were talking.

He said to her, "Your son still carries the spirit of a monk. He has been around the world on foot as a monk would do. He has traveled without money. He has been promoting the principles of peace and nonviolence. I am very impressed with his actions."

Listening to Gurudev, my mother's heart softened. Somehow she discovered that I was living in Varanasi. She made her way there and found me. I was still angry and resentful toward her. I could not forget the day when I was homeless, penniless, and vulnerable and my mother had rejected me.

"I have come to see you and ask your forgiveness" were my mother's first words. I was speechless. What could I say? What could I do?

"Although you left the monkhood, what you have done by going on a peace pilgrimage was the act of a monk. In any case, I regret my rejection of you. You are working for peace in the world. I have come to appreciate your achievements. I want to make peace with you. I have come to give you a mother's blessing."

This was all totally unexpected. Mother's sweet words made my heart melt. She had come alone all the way from Rajasthan, more than five hundred miles, changing trains twice. This was the first time she had been to Varanasi since she and I had scattered my father's ashes in the Ganges. Her humility and generosity touched my heart.

"Thank you, mother," I replied, "but these ten years have been very hard. I could find another guru, like Vinoba, I could find other friends, but I could not find another mother. Your rejection wounded me. I am pleased that you have come and you have forgiven me. I too forgive you for rejecting me. You not only gave me life, you gave me your wisdom, for that I am grateful to you." As I said these words, a river of tears was rolling down my mother's face. I too was crying. We hugged each other—the longest and tightest hug of my life.

When I left the monkhood, my guru Tulsi was extremely upset; in fact, more than upset, he was furious—which was unexpected in an accomplished and highly regarded spiritual teacher. Tulsi was not only my guru, he was also like my father. He had done everything to look after me, teach me, care for me. My leaving the order was a betrayal on two counts: I broke the sacred vow to remain a monk for life, and I was disloyal and ungrateful by rejecting Tulsi in favor of a mundane, worldly life.

Immediately after I left the monkhood, Tulsi sent his lay followers to seize me and to dissuade me from leaving. They tried to force me to return to the fold. Tulsi even tried to influence Vinoba not to let me become a member of his ashram. Fortunately, Vinoba ignored his efforts. But this kind of action made me even more rebellious, and I began campaigning against organized religion in general and my Jain sect in particular. I was caught in fierce antagonism with my guru for at least seven or eight years. Tulsi made it clear through his followers that he did not ever wish to see me again. It was a period of prolonged bitterness for both of us.

But time heals. Tulsi seemed to keep track of me and what I was doing. My walk around the world promoting peace softened his heart. He had praised me to my mother, and yet he never took any step toward reconciliation with me. But then neither did I. I thought we would never see each other again.

More time passed, I left India, married, and had a son called Mukti. When Mukti was in his twenties, he went to India to find his roots and to learn a little more about the land of his father. Without any prompting from me, and without my knowledge, he went to my birthplace and then to see Tulsi. When Tulsi realized that Mukti was my son, he was taken aback. After some conversation, Tulsi said, "Have you got pen and paper?"

"Yes, of course, sir" said Mukti.

"Please take a message from me to your father: 'What you have done and achieved is admirable. The past is past, all is forgiven. Come and see me.' Please take my request to your father," said Tulsi.

When Mukti returned home, he said to me, "Daddy, you have got to go and see your Guru, you must. He is getting old. I could see by his face that he is anxious to see you before he dies." This was powerful pleading from my son. The message from Guru was very touching too, so I said to Mukti, "All right, I will go and see him as soon as I can."

I was afraid to go on my own, so I asked my dear friend John Lane, who was an Indophile, if he would come with me and meet my guru. To my delight, he said yes. We flew to Delhi and took a train to the town of Ladnun where Tulsi was in residence.

In the late morning, John and I went to present ourselves to Tulsi. From the far end of a large hall, we could see him sitting on a raised dais addressing disciples and lay people. Since John was a big man and the only Westerner to enter the hall, we were noticed immediately. One of the organizers, on learning who I was, led us to the front, and we found ourselves beside Tulsi. He was completely surprised, yet pleased to see me.

"How long have you come for?" he asked.

"At least one day," I said.

"That's not enough. We have much to talk about. Stay here for a few days," Tulsi insisted. Then he said, "Much water has passed under the bridge." He paused. "How long ago was it that you left me?" he tried to remember.

"Nearly 40 years," I said.

"At that time I had great expectations of you. Everybody thought that you would make a wonderful teacher. Some people even suggested that you had the potential to be my heir. So not only I but everybody who knew you was more than disappointed. We felt betrayed. How could you do that? What more could we have done for you?"

Many monks and lay disciples listening to Tulsi were thinking the same. I was given so much love, care, training, and attention, and yet I expressed no gratitude and left them and my monkhood so abruptly.

I could hear the pain in his voice. Even though what I had done was so long ago, it was clear that the wounds had not healed. I remembered those days, and I remembered how much Tulsi had loved me.

"I am deeply and sincerely sorry that I abandoned you. I regret that I expressed no gratitude for all that you did for me. But thank you for inviting me to see you, and thank you for sending the message with my son, Mukti, that all is forgiven," I said.

We remained silent for a while. Then I continued, "Your teachings and your wisdom have informed my life. I have learned to live simply and lightly on the Earth. I have practiced detachment as you taught me. I have always remembered your words that love and attachment are not the same. I learned from you to trust myself, and trust the world. There are no words which can convey my indebtedness to you." I was in tears. John put his hand on my shoulder and passed me his handkerchief.

"You have done well," Tulsi said. "I have been informed of your adventures, your pilgrimages, and your commitment to making the world a better place. And if my teachings have been helpful to you, then I am delighted. I wish to bless you and wish you joy in your journey through life."

This was an act of great generosity and forgiveness on the part of my guru. I bowed to him again and again. John and I spent a couple of days in Tulsi's presence talking about the state of the world and how being nonviolent to Nature is an integral and distinctive contribution of Jain teachings.

"Nonviolence to oneself and nonviolence to people must be extended to nonviolence to all living beings. It is imperative that we honor not only the fundamental dignity of all human beings but of all living beings," Tulsi said with profound conviction. It was reassuring and healing for me to hear his teachings once more.

❦

Another wonderful example of forgiveness is Jo Berry. She is the daughter of Sir Anthony Berry, a Conservative Member of Parliament who was killed by the Irish Republican Army (IRA) in the Brighton hotel bombing in 1984, while attending the annual Conservative Party conference. Jo said to me that the trauma and grief of losing her father in such a shocking way made her think long and hard. "I can seek revenge or I can seek peace," she thought. She chose forgiveness in place of blame and hatred.

"The hardest bridge to build was with Patrick Magee, who planted the bomb which killed my father," she remembered. "After he was released from prison, I met him at a friend's house in Dublin. I was scared. At first he defended his political perspective, but then he started to hear my pain. Something changed. He had taken off his political hat, and his human heart opened. I said to him, 'Let us forgive each other. Whatever I do, nothing will bring my father back, but let us do something together so that no daughter or son loses their father in such violent circumstances in the future.'"

This was a true moment of reconciliation. Jo Berry, a victim of violence, forgave Patrick Magee, perpetrator of her father's death. From then on, they have worked together to build bridges for peace. They have spoken together at more than a hundred meetings, reaching people with their inspiring narrative. They remind their audiences that violence begets violence, revenge begets revenge. The only way forward is to forgive and forget and begin anew. As the saying goes:

The first to apologize is the bravest.
The first to forgive is the strongest.
The first to forget is the happiest.

How long can we carry the burden of the past? History is full of atrocities and cruelties, slavery, racism, colonialism, apartheid, the Holocaust, and genocide in one form or another.

Patrick Magee had been given eight life sentences. The judge branded him as a man of exceptional cruelty and inhumanity. In the end he served 14 years in prison and was released as part of the Good Friday agreement which brought an end to sectarian strife in Ireland. Now he is a transformed man devoting his entire life to planting the seeds of love in place of hate. It is said, "There is no love without forgiveness, and there is no forgiveness without love."

This story shows that good and bad runs through every human heart, and that every human being has the potential to be transformed. The power of compassion and forgiveness is greater than the power of punishment and revenge.

My final example of forgiveness is the work of the Truth and Reconciliation Commission of South Africa, which proved to be a supreme and unsurpassed example of peacemaking in the history of twentieth-century politics. The long and bitter struggle to end apartheid was led by many great activists, including Nelson Mandela who spent 27 years in prison. The history of the anti-apartheid movement is well recorded and well-known. What is remarkable in this amazing story is the victims' generosity of spirit. As president of the new South Africa, Nelson Mandela urged people to recognize and acknowledge the injustice, cruelty, and violence perpetrated by the apartheid regime and then to let go and move on. In order to achieve this, Mandela established the Truth and Reconciliation Commission under the chairmanship of Archbishop Desmond Tutu. To avoid victor's justice, no side was exempt from appearing before the Commission, and in the end, 849 people were granted amnesty and forgiveness.

As Bernard Meltzer, a US radio host, once said, "Forgiveness does not change the past, but it does change the future." This approach stands in contrast to that taken by the Nuremberg Trials. The reconciliatory approach has proven to be a successful way of dealing with the crimes of apartheid.

From my personal experience as well as the experience of socially and politically active campaigners, I have found ample evidence of resolving conflict through forgiveness, whereas revenge and punishment only exacerbate wounds and divisions and bring no healing. We have had enough of conflicts and wars. Now is the time for the people of the world to commit themselves to the way of negotiation. Negotiation and forgiveness is the way of the brave and courageous. As Mahatma Gandhi said, "The weak can never forgive, forgiveness is an attribute of the strong."

There have been many examples of conflicts and forgiveness within the context of human societies. Today the overwhelming conflict is between human greed and Earth's capacity. During the past few centuries, industrial societies have ravaged the Earth's resources, treating animals, forests, and oceans as mines from which to extract wealth. It seems that humanity is at war with Nature. We treat the land and pollute the biosphere as if we were at war. The mission of modern society appears to be to conquer Nature.

A time will come when humanity recognizes its folly and asks for forgiveness from the Earth. As yet, the majority of people have not recognized their stupidity and recklessness. They still believe it is their prerogative to use the natural world to meet the increasing demands of the worldwide consumer society. Although a growing minority of people around the world recognize that humans need to live simply within the limits of the finite Earth and consider themselves an integral part of Nature rather than her master, this view is still not mainstream. It may be some time before we realize this grave mistake. But sooner or later, the time will come when we need to ask for the Earth's forgiveness. I believe the Earth is bountiful and generous enough to forgive us, and we may be able to repair the damage we have caused. But if we don't realize our mistakes in time, then sadly but surely human survival will be in danger.

Increasingly, many people recognize that humanity has to live in harmony with the Earth. At the end of 2015, nearly two hundred world governments gathered together and unanimously agreed that due to human activities and particularly the excessive use of fossil fuels, the climate is changing, and this change will have a catastrophic impact on planet Earth and on the survival of human civilization as well as many species. Surprisingly, most world governments are now in the process of ratifying the Paris Agreement. If these governments stay true to their commitment and implement the policy of reducing their carbon emissions, that will be, in my view, a step towards asking forgiveness of the Earth.

On a nongovernmental level, many communities are taking actions to mitigate the damage human activities have inflicted upon the Earth. The Transition Town movement is an inspiring example of people taking responsibility for making the transition from a fossil fuel-based lifestyle to one based on renewable energy. The Transition movement claims to include nearly four hundred towns and communities around the world taking initiatives to moderate their dependence on exploitative and harmful systems. In Devon, where I live, Totnes was the first such town, and I have witnessed a change not only of attitudes but also of lifestyles in a way which establishes a more humble and grateful relationship with our planet home. This humility is in itself a way of asking forgiveness from the Earth.

Right relationship, radical love, and unconditional forgiveness are the fruits of a deep conviction that life is full of paradoxes, dilemmas, and choices pulling us in opposing directions. In such situations, we have to rise above the dialectics of opposites and reach out for a state of equilibrium through the practice of equanimity. By doing so, we will be better equipped to live a life of elegant simplicity. Let us join the dance of opposites in the next chapter.

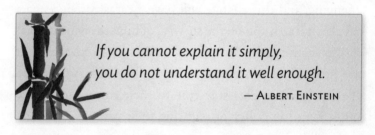

If you cannot explain it simply, you do not understand it well enough.
— ALBERT EINSTEIN

dance of opposites

Life and death are one
as the river and the sea are one.

Kahlil Gibran

SIMPLICITY OF THE MIND can only be accomplished through a sense of equanimity in all situations. The end of autumn and the beginning of winter is a special time, the threshold of the dark period. We should go into this winter season with an open mind and heart. We should welcome the darkness. This is a time for hibernation, a time for rest and rejuvenation. We should embrace the long nights. Sit by the fire, read stories, sing and dance together. These things can be done more easily when there is a dark period. Darkness is not something to be afraid of. When we have long days and light evenings, we want to go out walking or gardening, but when the evenings are long and dark, we can go into the sphere of the imagination. We can write poetry, or read *War and Peace*. Yes, light is welcome but dark is equally welcome. Lots of people talk about enlightenment. But we can also talk about endarkenment. This is the art of aligning the opposites.

When it is dark out in the woods, those of us who fear ghosts or nature spirits are afraid to go there. But there is no need to fear them. When we die, we will also become ghosts and join the nature spirits. Ghosts become friends when we are not afraid of them. Nature spirits, the human spirit, and ghosts are part of the same energy field. Ghosts do not communicate with everybody. If you are able to attract ghosts, then you have something special in your aura!

Whether or not you experience the presence of ghosts, we all have to live in the presence of the dark. We all need to befriend the dark. Only in the dark can we really recuperate. Darkness offers us a time of renewal. When I have worked in the light of day for many hours, I long for darkness. I turn off the lights and make the room dark. If there is light coming from the street, I draw the curtain to make the room darker. When windows, shutters, and doors are all closed, then I can relax. The last shutters to close are my eyelids, and when these are closed I sleep.

When we are asleep, our body regains the energy it has lost during the day. It is in the light that we spend energy — garden, cook, study, walk, work, and play. All day we use a lot of energy. We have to recuperate that energy. We can do so only in the dark.

Spiritual renewal also takes place in the dark. Mystics call it the dark night of the soul. When we go through emotional difficulties, psychological problems, or a spiritual crisis, then, metaphorically, we are in the dark night. If we can embrace this state of darkness with equanimity, then we come out of it stronger. During such "dark nights," we use our imagination, our faith, and meditation to face the crisis without a breakdown. Every crisis is an opportunity. We can use the crisis of our doubts and despondency to reconnect with our deeper selves.

Most of us have gone or will go through a personal or inner crisis. The first step in transforming the crisis into an opportunity is to recognize, "I am in a crisis." Being aware of one's state of mind is the beginning of the healing process. The next step is to allow oneself the time and space to meditate on the causes and conditions that have led to the crisis. Meditation is the best medicine for the mind. Etymologically the words *meditation* and *medicine* derive from the same Latin root, *midure*, which means "to pay attention." When we need to pay attention to our bodies, we take some medicine, when we need to pay attention to our minds, we meditate. Paying attention is a step toward awareness of ourselves and awareness of the causes of our crisis. Then we soon realize that the root causes of our inner crisis are ego, ambition, desire to control, clinging to our material or intellectual possessions, and craving for power, position, money, and status.

The planetary crisis has similar causes. Humankind has come to believe that we can control Nature, that we can rule over oceans and forests, rivers, and animals. Yes, we can land on the moon, we can build nuclear weapons. But in our deep meditation, we realize that we are not so powerful. We are not as powerful as a tornado or as strong as a hurricane. Even a heavy rainfall can put us in our place. We need to be humble and respect the power of Nature. To address the environmental crisis, we need to be in harmony with the natural world. We are not in charge of the Earth, we are not in control of Nature. It is time we learned to practice humility.

As we have tsunamis and storms in the outer world, sometimes we have tsunamis and storms in our inner world. At these times we need to develop compassion for ourselves and for planet Earth. Sweeping the crisis under the carpet is no solution. Any crisis is a call for attention. We need to address it with grace and gratitude. All crises, be they outer or inner, come from disconnection. The resolution of these crises is reconnection. In meditation we need to focus on our deep and unshakeable unity and connectivity with the outer world of Nature and people as well as the inner world of the soul.

In India, when we meet each other, we put our two hands together and say, "Namaste." Which means "I bow to you." When we put our palms together, we create a union. We make two into one. As two palms become one, you and I become one. The opposites come together. The duality of one is the unity of two. What appears to be opposite is in reality complementary. As above, so below. Masculine and feminine complement each other as do dark and light, negative and positive. The opposites together create wholeness and completeness. If the year was all summer and bright light, it would be boring. It is good that we have dark winters to balance. This is the beautiful design of Nature. Every season is good; together they make the whole.

Health is important, but there is meaning in illness too. Only a living body can have a headache; a dead body cannot have a headache. When we are ill, we have a chance to sleep, to rest, to slow down. If someone is ill, it gives the family a chance to come together, to help and care for the patient and for each other. If we were never ill, and never needed anybody, nobody would have the opportunity to help us. Illness is a dark period. It is an opportunity to go to bed and let the body heal itself.

We function between two landscapes: the outer landscape of the physical and natural world, and the inner landscape of the metaphysical and spiritual world. We live among trees, rivers, and mountains where we endure storms, floods, and earthquakes. Similarly we live in our mind, emotions, and feelings, where we experience crises of anger, fear, doubt, despondency, and depression. As we live in the outer landscape of natural beauty, we also live in the inner landscape of love. We need to accept bewilderment and certainty, doubt and faith, darkness and light, confusion and clarity, rough and smooth, pain and pleasure, gain and loss, success and failure. When we can accept everything and cultivate equanimity, then we are able to sail through the sea of life with great ease.

This is the dance of life symbolized by yin and yang, a circle half black and half white. In the black there is a spot of white, and in the white there is a spot of black. It is a perfect symbol of wholeness. Nothing is wholly dark and nothing is wholly light. Therefore when we are in the light, we should remember the dark, and when we are in the dark, we should remember the light. In Indian iconography, there is a divine form which is half male, Shiva, and half female, Shakti, the yin and yang in one body. Every man has feminine in him, and every woman has masculine in her. Masculine and feminine principles act together. They dance together. This is the movement of dark and light, inner and outer, masculine and feminine, matter and spirit. It is a manifestation of equilibrium. The universe is in this dance of opposites.

Birth and death together make the wholeness of life. Death brings renewal. We need never be afraid of death. Never think that death is bad, or painful, or difficult. Death is liberating and transformative. Death is not the end of life. Death is the door into new life. Spirit is eternal. Life is eternal. Then why should we fear death? As we welcome spring and birth, we should welcome winter and death.

As a young boy of four, I was shocked by the death of

my father. At age nine, I left home to seek a death-free existence, but now I realized that without death there is no birth. Death is not a negative, death is as imperative as birth.

From birth we begin to climb the Mount Everest of life, at death we reach the peak. How can we fear reaching the peak? Death is liberation; we are freed from our ailing and aging body. We are freed from anger, anxiety, and anguish, from pride, prejudice, and passions, from doubt, depression, and despair. Why should we not be glad to embrace such freedom?

My mother would say, "When you feel fragile and weak and you sense your life is ending, then instead of waiting for death to meet you, you go to meet death." When she was past 80, quite frail, and unable to see or hear very well, she said, "No, I don't want glasses or a hearing aid." One morning she took her walking stick in her hand and went to her daughters and sons and said to them, "From today I am going to fast unto death. If I have said anything which was hurtful or if I have done anything that was unpleasant, I have come to ask your forgiveness." She asked for pardon from her friends and extended family. Then she came home and remained in her room. The news spread: "Anchi Devi is fasting to death." People came from far and wide, they sat near her, singing sacred songs. They thanked her for her kindness. For nearly a month, she lived on boiled water. During this time, there was celebration, music, chanting, people asking for forgiveness, people giving forgiveness, and saying goodbye. Thus she died peacefully and happily.

Her body was placed on a beautiful palanquin. There was a procession to the cremation ground. Whatever money she had left was distributed amongst the poor. The

funeral pyre was built of nine different kinds of wood, including sandalwood and coconut to create a good aroma.
The fire was lit by her eldest son, and everyone stayed until
the body turned to ashes. The next day her family collected
the ashes, which later were scattered in the Ganges. Her
ashes dissolved in the waters of the river, flowed into the
ocean, evaporated into the clouds, then fell as rain on the
soil. Thus every part of her was recycled. My mother's body
had become part of the universe, part of the cycle of life
and death.

At the age of 88, my teacher Vinoba Bhave developed
a severe stomach ulcer. His friends took him to hospital.
The doctor examined him and said, "This is a very advanced
ulcer, we can operate on it, but we only have a 50/50 chance
of success. You need to give us permission to operate."
Vinoba said, "At my age I don't want to go through such a
big operation. I will fast unto death." He was so frail that
he only lasted seven days. But those seven days were full
of celebration. The Prime Minister of India, Mrs. Indira
Gandhi, came to pay homage to him while he was fasting.
Fifty thousand people came to his funeral. At that season,
the great river Paramdham which flowed past Vinoba's ashram was dry, so the river bed, where his body was cremated,
was full of people. Later, during the monsoon, the river
flowed again and carried Vinoba's ashes to the sea.

Fasting unto death is a remarkable way of dying and has
the full support of the Hindu and Jain religious communities. The Gita says that if old clothes are worn out, what do
we do? We discard the old and change into new. The body
is like a garment, when it is old and frail, it dies, and then we

take a new body. The spirit never dies. Only through death is life renewed.

In the Indian tradition, we do not have the idea that death is bad and life is good and therefore we must keep people alive at all costs. Death is as good as life, and life is a good as death. Birth and death are complementary; they are two sides of the same coin. If there is no birth, there is no death; and if there is no death, there is no birth. On the journey of life, there is the point of birth, arrival into this life, and the point of death, which is departure from this life. Coming and going are a continuum. As Eckhart Tolle said, "Life is not the opposite of death, the opposite of death is birth." Birth and death are a dance of the opposites on the stage of eternal life.

When we burn wood in a fireplace, the wood gives its life to keep us warm; it dies and becomes ash. We put that ash around a tree. The ash is composted and transformed into soil. Then the soil is transformed into the tree. The tree grows, matures, and falls. It becomes a tree again. Actually the wood never really died, it only kept transforming itself. That same wood ash could have been put on a bed of potatoes. Then the ash would have nourished the seed potatoes and multiplied into many potatoes. Wood ash nourished potatoes, potatoes nourished we humans. Now we are wood reborn as humans.

The word *human* comes from *humus* which means "soil." Human beings are soil beings. Immortal life manifests itself in mortal, material forms which move in the eternal cycle of time, space, and consciousness. Nothing is static, fixed, or rigid. Everything is dynamic and cyclical. Existence is eternal, but all physical forms are impermanent and ever-changing. What appears opposite, binary, contradictory, and complicated are in truth complementary and conciliatory. In order to understand and appreciate this simple truth, we need to see beyond the superficial.

For me, life is simple, why do we make it so complicated? We do not need to make life difficult for ourselves by engaging in apparent disconnections and divisions. We can simply relax in the realization that the diversity of matter is rooted in the unity of spirit. This deeper reality can be experienced through deep seeing. In the next chapter, we will explore the meaning of deep seeing.

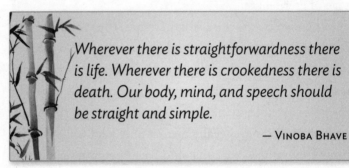

Wherever there is straightforwardness there is life. Wherever there is crookedness there is death. Our body, mind, and speech should be straight and simple.

— VINOBA BHAVE

deep seeing

To see clearly
is poetry, prophecy,
and religion, all in one.

John Ruskin

To LIVE SIMPLY is to see deeply. There is a great deal of difference between watching, looking, and seeing. What is called *darshan* in Sanskrit could be translated as *deep seeing*—seeing that which lies beyond appearances.

When I was young, I would go for the darshan of Guru Tulsi, my Jain teacher. A monk in Sanskrit is called *muni*, which means "one who keeps silence," and the disciple is called *shrawak* which means "one who listens." The teacher is silent and the disciple listens. There is a subtle connection between deep listening and deep seeing. When we listen in silence, we develop the ability to see with our third eye. We listen beyond sound to listen to the soundless, and we go beyond form to see the formless. Generally we see things with our two eyes, and we hear words with our two ears, but monks are trained to see beyond images and to listen beyond words.

When I went for darshan, I would sit facing the guru. Not a single word would be communicated for about an hour. I would just sit. If I wasn't with my guru, then I might sit in front of a statue of a deity in a temple. I would sit and meditate. The *shrawak* listens to the sacred sound of Om without any words. Simply a sound reverberating within. At the beginning of the practice, I would chant Om out loud, but soon I was instructed to drop the articulation of the sound and listen to the echo of Om within my being.

Darshan is to see the image beyond the physical form, to experience the ineffable—pure peace, pure light, and pure energy. This process is akin to the work of an artist. When artists paint or draw, they see the subject deeply, they see something beyond the physical form. As a consequence, the separation between the subject and the artist disappears. The observer and the observed become one. In this state the artist becomes a "seer," a sage. A seer is practicing darshan. A seer is called *darshanik*—the one who gives and the one who receives darshan. In darshan there is no separation between the deity and the devotee, between the guru and the disciple, the outer god and the inner god, the outer guru and the inner guru.

A true seer is able to see with the third eye, like that of Lord Shiva, which means the power to see beyond the material world into the nonmaterial world of the formless. Going from form to formless and back into form is a spiritual journey.

Buddhists say, "Gate, gate, paragate, parsamgate, Bodhi Swaha," which means "gone and gone again, gone beyond, gone utterly beyond, into enlightenment." Through deep seeing, the world of superficiality dissolves. The authentic world of true reality emerges. At this point there is radiance, from the unity of matter and spirit. This deep seeing ends all dualities and divisions.

The one who is able to see totally and fully without becoming entangled in the dualities of the world is a visionary. The visionary sees with the eye of wisdom, the eye of the heart, the poetic eye. Jonathan Swift said, "Vision is the art of seeing what is invisible to others." Poets see it all because they are seeing with the eye of the imagination, the third eye.

Wisdom comes from deep seeing and deep experience. With our intellect, we acquire knowledge; with our ears and eyes, we acquire information, but with the third eye we experience unity and equanimity.

With words and images, we can grasp a partial truth, but when we close our eyes and mouths and go beyond intellect, we open ourselves to the possibility of experiencing the whole truth. Knowledge without experience is profane and superficial. Knowledge with experience enables us to look at the world and see it whole and sacred. There is plenty of knowledge in the world today, but there is little sense of the sacred, little sense of wholeness. Highly educated people often have no sense of the sacred, no wisdom, or compassion. Knowledge built on the foundation of darshan enables humanity to function holistically with reverence and wisdom. Darshan delivers the insight that animal life, plant life, rock life, river life, human life, all life is sacred.

Universities teach academic knowledge, factual information and data, without vision. Academics are rarely visionaries; they are well-read, but there are very few seers among them. They need to close their books and shut down their screens, then close their eyes and visualize the wholeness of life, seeing with the eye of the heart that everything is interconnected, interrelated, and interdependent. Through darshan we look at the world and see it whole.

When we only see with our two eyes, we see everything as separate. The tree is separate from the soil, the bird sitting on a branch is separate from the tree, the bees buzzing around are separate from the flowers, human beings are separate from Nature. Such superficial perception has created the story of separation. A new story is the story of union and reunion of all life.

Seers perceive trees and birds as related. The birds eat

the fruit from the trees and nest in them, the birds cannot exist if there are no trees. The trees are nourished by the compost of the bird droppings. Bees cannot exist if there are no flowers, and without pollination by the bees, the flowers cannot exist.

Humans cannot exist without trees. How can we survive without the oxygen-carbon cycle of trees? Trees work day and night for us. If trees and bees did not exist, humans would not exist either. No bees, no pollination, no food, no life. Einstein said, "If bees disappear from this world, human life will not survive for more than four years." Einstein was a seer, he saw the existential unity of life.

Everything coexists. Because everything is made of same elements—earth, air, fire, and water—so we are one. By seeing deeply, we realize that we are all related. We are in a bond of relationships, and we break those bonds at our peril. We have a sacred bond with trees, bees, birds, rivers, mountains, and forests. We have a sacred bond even with the earthworms! They work under the soil day and night. If the worms were not there, there would be no food on our table. Earthworms actually work 24 hours a day to keep the soil in good heart. They do this without pay and without holidays, to keep the soil fertile. We plant the seed because the soil is made ready by the earthworms to grow our food and to give us nourishment. An Indian scientist has calculated that one earthworm turns six tons of soil in its lifetime. It shows that if we have enough earthworms we hardly need rotovators or tractors!

Earthworms help to produce food to nourish our bodies, but we also need food to nourish our souls. A sense of the sacred, a sense of the unity of life and compassion for all living beings nourishes the soul. Nourishment of the soul and nourishment of the body are linked. If our body is not nourished, our soul cannot be nourished, if our soul is not nourished, our body will not be.

We know this truth through darshan, through deep observation. This is how all philosophies and all sciences developed. Observation requires patience, we have to slow down. Newton had to wait until the apple matured on the tree, until it ripened. When the apple was ripe, it liberated itself from the branch easily and fell. Newton observed it with full attention and discovered gravity.

The Buddha, like Newton, also showed great patience. He too sat under a tree, observing it for a long time. Clouds came and brought rain to give nourishment to the tree, and birds came to shelter there and to eat from its fruit. The Buddha observed that the tree gave fruit to everyone without any discrimination. He saw unconditional compassion, love, and generosity embodied in the tree. The Buddha discovered compassion by observing a tree!

The tree laden with fruit never asks, "Have you come with your credit card?" Whoever comes to the tree, fruit is freely given. Young or old, rich or poor, black or white, saint or sinner, man or woman, human or animal, bird or wasp, all are welcome. All can have fruit.

When the Buddha sat under the tree, he observed this interrelatedness of the whole and he experienced the darshan of Nature. He saw that Nature is sacred. The fruit sacrifices itself to give nourishment to humans, to animals, to birds, to bees, and to wasps. That is why trees are sacred. That is why they are called the tree of life, the tree of knowledge, the tree of wisdom, the speaking tree. The tree communicated in silence. The Buddha heard its wisdom. By deep observation, by deep seeing, by taking darshan of the tree, the Buddha was enlightened.

Darshan transforms the ordinary into the extraordinary. If we see a tree only with our two eyes, we see only wood and branches, leaves and flowers. A useful processing mechanism for oxygen and carbon dioxide, and good for firewood. But if we see a tree with our third eye, that ordinary tree is transformed into a sacred tree. Then the tree becomes our teacher. A seeker of enlightenment can sit under a tree and find self-realization. Darshan transforms a mountain or river into a god or a goddess, the earth becomes heaven, a piece of stone becomes a sculpture, a living Shiva, and an image in wood becomes an enlightened Buddha.

Darshan transforms our consciousness, our whole way of seeing the world. Theologian Thomas Berry experienced darshan when he said, "The universe is not a collection of objects, it is a communion of subjects." God is not someone separate from us who worked for six days and created the world, then on the seventh day went to sleep. The Hindu idea of god is that the universe itself is an embodiment of god, a dance of Shiva, a cosmic play. We cannot separate the dancer from the dance. The whole universe is divine. Every leaf, every blade of grass, every worm, every wasp, every flower, every fruit, every child, everything is a divine dance. Emerson said, "Never lose an opportunity of seeing anything beautiful, for beauty is god's handwriting."

William Blake was in the mood of darshan when he wrote, "To see the world in a grain of sand and heaven in a wild flower, hold infinity in the palm of your hand and eternity in an hour." Blake looked at a grain of sand and saw the whole world in it! The metaphysical dimension is not separate from the physical dimension, physical and metaphysical are two aspects of one single reality. With two eyes we see the physical, and with the third eye we imagine and see the metaphysical. Rumi said, "Stop acting so small, you are the universe in ecstatic motion."

Darwin studied earthworms which led to further research into the nature of living creatures. Through deep observation, he saw that all living beings have evolved from the same source and thus we are all connected. This was as much a spiritual insight as an intellectual and rational realization.

In the modern world, learning has been reduced to measurement. What can be measured matters; what cannot be measured does not exist. This is what most people believe because their vision is limited to physical reality. This is why we need darshan, to see something beyond physical and measurable reality; to see the spiritual dimension. Matter and spirit are not separate; there is no division. Spirit and matter are entangled. Matter cannot exist without being imbued with spirit. My body would be useless if it was not a living body. The human spirit makes the human body come alive. We become animated, we become part of *anima mundi*, the universal soul. Soul and body together make us who we are. If there is no soul, no spirit, no imagination, then the mere body is a dead body. The only thing to do with it is put it in a coffin. Matter needs spirit in order to be animated. Spirit needs matter to manifest itself. Soul, spirit, imagination, and consciousness are the metaphysical reality which works through the physical reality.

I could not write if I did not have these two hands to

hold the pen and move it on paper. Yet hands by themselves cannot write, they need the imagination. But the body and the imagination are not two separate things. There is no dualism, they are totally entangled. Those who are only materialists are missing something, and those who are only spiritualists are also missing something. But those who can see with the third eye can see the unity of spirit and matter. The theoretical physicist David Bohm called it wholeness and the implicate order.

With wholeness comes healing. Without wholeness there is no healing. When we are broken, separated, and divided, we are ill. When we are whole, then we are healed. When we are healed, then we are happy. The purpose of life is to be happy. And to be happy is to be whole. It is as simple as that. But knowing how to be happy is not that simple. So we need darshan, deep insight, to know how to be happy and how to transform every action into a source of happiness.

For example, cooking need not be a chore, it can be a joy. When I go into the kitchen I say, "Ahh, I am going to do some cooking, what a pleasure! I will prepare something delightful." Going into the garden is the same, "Wow! What a wonderful day. The sun is shining, I'm going to breathe fresh air, touch the soil, plant some seeds, and smell the flowers." The moment we start to take joy in our action, the action becomes a source of happiness. Life is transformed. We can rise above the duality of good and bad and arrive at a state of equanimity.

Rumi said, "Somewhere beyond the ideas of right and wrong, there is a field. I will meet you there." This is a perfect example of darshan. With darshan even in difficult times, we are in a state of bliss. A person of darshan takes the rough with the smooth and considers the rough and the smooth as part of each other. Leonard Cohen sang about this truth: "There is a crack, a crack in everything / that's how the light gets in."

In this chapter, I have explored the simple but profound idea of darshan which helps us to bridge the dichotomy of dualism—dualism of physical and metaphysical, of material and spiritual, of rough and smooth. But one of the most bothersome dichotomies is that of science and spirituality. If we are well equipped with the idea of darshan, we can overcome this duality without difficulty. In the next chapter, I will address this complex question of the relationship between science and spirituality and look for some simple answers.

A cluttered house is a sign of a cluttered life and cluttered mind.

— R. D. LAING

union of science and spirituality

Science is not only compatible
with spirituality;
it is a profound source
of spirituality.

Carl Sagan

In order to embody the philosophy of elegant simplicity, we need to address the relationship between science and spirituality. Some people think that science and spirituality are polar opposites, but are they? Science is about things which can be measured, and spirituality is about things which cannot be measured. In life, both of these are integrated together. Look at our bodies. We can measure the weight, length, width, structure, and anatomy of the body. But we also have intelligence. How do we measure intelligence? We can do some IQ tests, but we can never really measure how much intelligence we have. Then we have feelings, like love for our friends and family. Can we measure love? So spirituality is about what cannot be measured. We need to measure what can be measured, but we also need to accept the truth that there are dimensions of life which cannot be measured.

There are scientific theories such as complexity, chaos, Gaia and evolution which come close to spirituality. Quantum physics in particular bridges the gap between meaning and measurement. When you put meaning into quantity, quantity becomes quantum. At quantum level, all separations end. We are all related and connected at the energy level. Thus the meaning of existence is unmanifest and invisible and therefore spiritual. Some of my scientist friends believe that consciousness is close to quantum physics because at the level of quantum mechanics all manifestation is potential. The meaning of consciousness is also the same; there is an unmanifest potential before reality manifests. In the spiritual terminology, we call it consciousness, in scientific terminology, we call it quantum mechanics.

We can measure matter, but we cannot measure meaning. When I write an article, I can say it is eight hundred words and will fit on one page. I can count the number of words, and I can measure how much space it will take, but the meaning of the words and the quality of the writing cannot be measured. I can feel the meaning and sense it, but I cannot measure it. Words have a physical reality, but their meaning is metaphysical. The law has two aspects: the letter of the law and the spirit of the law. Everything has a physical reality and a metaphysical reality. We have the human body and the human spirit. We need matter and we need spirit. They form one unified reality. One cannot exist without the other. There is no separation or dualism between the physical and the metaphysical or between the material and the spiritual.

Science gives us rational, logical, empirical, measurable, and replicable tools and technologies which we need to function well in life. Spirituality gives us love, compassion, generosity, and a sense of mutuality. We need these too.

Without the spiritual dimension of values, vision, ethics, and aesthetics, science can lead us astray. When there are no values to guide it, science ends up producing nuclear weapons. If spirituality guided the actions of scientists, then they would think ten times before inventing weapons of war and other tools of destruction. Why do we have global warming? Because scientists have been working in the interests of the commercial and industrial establishments, without the guidance of spiritual values; that is why their scientific and technological innovations have led to planetary crises such as climate change.

Modern agriculture, for example, is scientific, yet it produces something like 18 percent of greenhouse gases. If agriculture was informed by spiritual values, it would be a very different situation.

Spiritual agriculture such as biodynamic farming, agro–ecology, and permaculture emphasize the value of the living soil and biodiversity. Whereas industrial "scientific" agriculture values nothing other than the quantity of food produced with the minimum input of labor. Modern agriculture uses combine harvesters, huge tractors, fertilizers, herbicides, pesticides, and genetically engineered seeds because it lacks the spiritual values of reverence for soil and animals. In scientific farming, food is no longer sacred. It is simply a commodity for profit. No wonder that millions of cows, pigs, and chickens are kept in the cruel conditions of factory farms where they never see the light of day in their whole lives. This is just one example of science and technology deprived of a spiritual ethos producing harmful results. We certainly need spiritual values in our agriculture!

Although there are scientists who embrace spirituality and work for the good of all, much of science has been in the service of greed, war, waste, pollution, exploitation, and injustice. This must change if science is to serve the interest and needs of humanity and planet Earth.

Einstein, one of the greatest scientists of the twentieth century, said, "Science without religion is blind, religion without science is lame." If we have no science, then we limp. We can see what is good, but we cannot implement our vision. Therefore the people of spirit and religion need to embrace science.

People who have developed deep spirituality have often been reluctant to address the problems of the material world. Things are now slowly changing, but for a long time, some societies were good at meditation and yoga, philosophy and poetry, but without scientific research and methodology, they suffered hunger, deprivation, and material poverty. So spirituality without science is truly lame.

Spirituality and religion without science often give rise to fundamentalism. Hindu, Buddhist, Christian, or Islamic fundamentalism is born whenever they reject scientific, rational, measured, and logical thinking. Spirituality without empiricism suffers from blind faith. People of blind faith don't see or believe in anything other than what is in their holy book. They take every word in the Bible or the Koran, the Torah or the Gita as the word of God. They think that there is only one truth and that they have that truth. Everybody must follow their truth. They deny the multiplicity and diversity of truths. They become missionaries and work hard to convert people of other religions to their religion. Of course, there are big-hearted and generous religious people, who embrace a scientific outlook, but they are in a small minority. Institutionalized religions largely suffer from dogmatism, fundamentalism, and exclusivism because they are unwilling to accept and respect the diversity of truths and the diversity of religions.

So science needs spirituality and spirituality needs science. They need each other. And there is no contradiction. There is no conflict between science and spirituality. Science complements spirituality and spirituality complements science. Spirituality give us vision and values. Science gives us tools and technologies. We need both. This is a holistic and inclusive way of thinking in which everything has a place, as long as they are in the right proportion and balance. For example, day and night have the right balance. Even though in summer there are long days and in winter there are long nights, overall there is a balance. The same kind of balance is needed between science and spirituality. In order to achieve this balance, people of faith and scientists all need a shot of humility and generosity.

Spirituality and religious experiences have nothing to do with any particular belief system. Believing means closing the mind. The moment I say "I believe in God," or "I believe in reincarnation," or "I believe in the Resurrection," or "I believe in the virgin birth," or this, that, or the other, I have closed my mind.

Spirituality is about love, not beliefs. Spiritual seekers are always on a journey, on a pilgrimage, seeking truth and enlightenment. There is no place where they can say "I have found the answer." Spirituality is a process, an exploration, not a destination. The same is true of science, it is an ever-evolving quest. Scientists search for the truth. They don't say "This is the end, we have arrived at our destination, there is no more research needed." Unfortunately, some scientists do say "Darwin was the last word." They close their minds and become believers. If you become a believer, you stop using your intelligence and your perceptions to learn from the world around you and from the experiences that you have. Then you have left the path of science *and* the path of spirituality.

Through science, as well as through spirituality, we are always looking for new insights and new wisdom, which can free us from dogmas, rigidities, and fixed beliefs. Science and spirituality, physics and metaphysics, chemistry and compassion, mind and matter can and must dance together.

For this dance to occur, I have formulated a trinity for our times. So that humanity can live in harmony with Nature, care for our human soul, and establish peace and justice worldwide, among all human communities, we need to give our attention to *soil*, *soul*, and *society*. Some time ago, I wrote a book of the same title, and as my ideas have developed further, I will give an overview of these ideas in the final chapter.

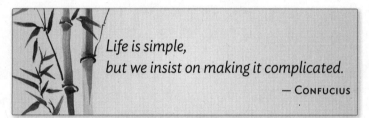

Life is simple,
but we insist on making it complicated.
— Confucius

soil, soul, and society

We live in an
interconnected world
and in an
interconnected time
so we need holistic
solutions to our
interconnected problems.

Naomi Klein

TO LIVE A LIFE of elegant simplicity, we need to pay attention to three areas of existence: our soil, our soul, and our society.

In every age, three words have been used to capture the spirit of the time. The motto of the French Revolution was *Liberté, egalité, fraternité*. That captured the essence of the revolution. It was a good trinity, but it didn't mention the human-Nature relationship; it made no mention of spirituality either. It was only a social and political trinity.

The Christian tradition has a spiritual trinity: Father, Son, and Holy Spirit. It makes no connection with any social dimension. And it leaves out the ecological dimension. The new age also has a trinity—mind, body, spirit—which does not address our relationship with Nature or our relationship with the human world. It's a personal trinity— my mind, my body, my spirit—and all about keeping them healthy and in balance.

There is also the American trinity: life, liberty, and the pursuit of happiness. But it is about human life, human liberty, and the pursuit of human happiness. When I go to the USA, I say to people, "You have been pursuing happiness for hundreds of years. Why don't you just *be* happy, rather than pursuing happiness!"

These trinities express the needs of the people at a particular historical moment. Now we are in the age of ecology. The twenty-first century is the century of ecology. The

twentieth century was the century of the economy. Free
trade, WTO, globalization, World Bank, IMF, and multi-
national corporations were the leading forces. All governments became obsessed with economics. Schools and
universities prepared young people to fit into the economic
system. The consequences of this economic paradigm for
the environment have been catastrophic. Planet Earth is in
a dire state. So the twenty-first century has to be the century of ecology. Governments and the media, industry and
educational establishments are beginning to pay attention
to the rainforests, to wilderness, to water and soil. So for
the century of ecology, we need a new trinity. And it should
be a holistic trinity. It must include ecological, spiritual, and
social dimensions. Therefore I offer a new trinity for our
times: Soil, soul, and society.

In Latin, soil is *humus*. From this root, we get human
and humility. When I say I am a human being, it means I
am of the soil, of the earth. Therefore we humans are not
superior to soil, we are made of soil. Soil is truly humble;
it always stays under our feet, never over our head. As soil
is humble, humans also need to be humble. When we lose
our humility, we lose our humanity. Being one with Nature,
with the Earth, and with the soil is our foremost quality of
being human.

Urban civilization has disconnected humans from
humus, from soil. The word *civilization* comes from *civic*
which is related to city. In Europe we have a civilization
which developed in cities like Florence, Vienna, Prague,
Venice, Paris, Rome, and London. In Sanskrit, the language
of ancient India, there is no word for "civilization." What we
have is *culture*, which developed in fields and forests. Great

books of philosophy, poetry, and stories were written by sages, poets, and philosophers who lived in the forests. Indian culture is a forest culture. It is rooted in the soil. In fact the word *culture* in Old English meant "soil."

Since the Renaissance and the Age of Enlightenment, we have developed a worldview in which human beings are the pinnacle of evolution. Our urban civilization assumes that land, animals, oceans, rivers, and forests exist simply to serve human needs, that Nature is there for human use and human benefit. When we look at the soil-based cultures of indigenous peoples, or at Taoist, Buddhist, and Hindu cultures, we find that human beings considered themselves to be as much part of the natural world as any other species.

Just as racism and nationalism narrow our thinking, so does speciesism. We start to demand special privileges and rights for humans above other species. To be holistic and ecological, we have to be free of speciesism.

Speciesism is the idea that human species are the only conscious and living species and other species have no soul and therefore human species are superior. This idea encourages us to believe that soil is without soul, that Earth is a dead rock, and Nature is unconscious. This is a fundamental error of our urban civilization. Traditional cultures all over the world believe that Nature is alive and that there is something called Nature spirit. Soil is soulful.

We use the soil to grow our food, make our clothes, and build our houses. During this process, soil is depleted. It is then our duty to replenish the soil by putting compost on it, or by leaving it fallow for a year or more.

Soil is a metaphor for all environmental and natural relationships. Everything comes from the soil. Forests, food, houses, clothes come from the soil. Our bodies come from the soil and return to the soil. Soil is the source of life. Three inches of topsoil maintains all life. If soil was not there, there would be no life. If we protected the soil and took care of her, everything else would take care of itself. Soil provides the greatest sequestration of carbon. Carbon is held beautifully in the soil. At the moment, the soil is denuded of carbon, because we dig it, plough it, and exploit it without limit. We hardly put any carbon back. Therefore the soil is becoming lifeless. If we can make the soil rich, put compost on her, and treat her gently, neither dig too much nor leave her too exposed, then carbon and fertility will be restored. To store carbon in the soil is a very wonderful way to mitigate the effects of climate change. Soil can store carbon even more than trees; this is the beauty of the soil.

In her book, *Soil Not Oil*, Vandana Shiva explains the qualities of soil and how it is literally the ground of all existence. Since becoming dependent on oil, we have forgotten the soil. Many things nowadays are made from oil. Our clothes of nylon and polyester are made from oil. Our food is produced with oil. Transportation, heating, lighting, and much else depends on oil. We have become not only dependent but addicted to a finite source. What will happen when oil runs out? We chant the mantra of oil, oil, oil. Oil and coal, all fossil fuels, are dark energy; they come from the underworld. We need to shift from this hellish energy to heavenly energy, solar, wind, and water energy. We should revalue soil. If we go from oil to soil, we and planet Earth will have a long life.

Once I went to visit Lady Eve Balfour, author of *The Living Soil*. She was the founder of the Soil Association.

She took me around her garden. It was late April. The garden was flourishing, flowers and vegetables in full bloom, whereas other gardens were struggling at that time of year. I asked her, "What is the secret of such a wonderful garden? What do you do?" Lady Eve replied, "I do nothing, I just take care of the soil. The soil takes care of the rest."

Soil is the key. John Vidal, environment editor at *The Guardian* newspaper, writes: "As a direct result of soil erosion, possibly 30 percent of the world's arable land has become unproductive in just 40 years, leading to severe decline in bird and animal life. Soil is the most precious of all resources, yet in one country after another, it is being allowed to wash or blow away."

Modern society does not value soil. It values oil, money, industry, infrastructure, but not soil. Soil is not on any government agenda. Look at the speeches made by parliamentarians and politicians—millions of words but the word *soil* will hardly be there. The prime ministers and presidents of the world rarely talk about soil. Even ministers of agriculture rarely talk about soil. Even ministers of the environment don't talk about the importance of soil. The media, schools, universities, business leaders seldom mention the word *soil*. But we must talk about soil. We must talk about putting compost on the soil, we must protect the fertility of the soil. We must learn to love the soil. Soil is the queen of the entire natural world.

Similarly we need to replenish our soul. We are always using our soul qualities while speaking, thinking, and feeling. Whenever we are anxious or happy, joyful or fearful, we use the energy of the soul. So we need to find ways of replenishing and healing the soul, the psyche. This is why all spiritual traditions have developed different techniques for healing the soul.

Meditation is one such technique. Meditation is a way of mindful living. It means to be attentive, to be calm, to be composed, to be silent, to be still, and to live in equanimity. If we are aware of the state of our mind, then we can be resilient and steadfast. We can go through difficult times with inner strength. We develop compassion, kindness, and generosity. These qualities bring joy, fulfillment, and happiness to our lives.

In meditation the outer world and the inner world meet. Soil and soul unite. Body and mind, matter and spirit integrate. Spiritual work and social work come together. Some people say, "Oh, I am an activist. I don't have time for meditation, I don't have time for spiritual practice. I just want to be an activist." Being an activist is good, but to be effective activists, we need to be strong within ourselves. Without inner resilience, outer activism cannot be sustained for long and we will soon burn out. When we look at the great activists, we find that they were also engaged in spiritual practice. Martin Luther King and Mahatma Gandhi are two of the many examples of activists who combine spirituality with political and social activism. No matter how busy Gandhi was, he never missed morning and evening mediations. Martin Luther King never missed his prayers. Meditation and prayer is to take time for oneself. If we do not take care of ourselves, who is going to take care of us? Why would we expect somebody else to take care of us if we neglect ourselves?

Taking care of yourself is not selfish. When you feed yourself, you are strengthened, and then you can go out and feed others. Do you ever say, "Oh, I don't have time for lunch, I am working to save the world"? No. Save the world, of course, but save yourself first. When you are in an airplane and there is an emergency, you are required to put an oxygen mask on yourself first, then take care of your neighbor. Taking care of yourself is a prerequisite for being able to take care of others. Others are none other than yourself. Taking care of yourself doesn't mean that you are being self-centered.

You are a microcosm of the macrocosm. The whole universe is within your "self." This is big mind thinking. *Anima mundi.* The soul of the universe. The universal soul and our personal soul are not separate. They are connected. The soul of the universe is the ultimate, the anima of the individual is the intimate. If we don't take care of the intimate, how can we take care of the ultimate? So the ultimate and the intimate are two aspects of one reality. That is why environmentalists and peacemakers need to pay attention to their personal well-being; they need to take care of the soul.

There's soul in the soil, there's soul in the tree. There's soul in everything. We have forgotten this truth. As soil is the key to the external landscape, soul is the key to the internal landscape. Thomas Moore, an American psychologist and author of *Care of the Soul,* maintains that the human soul is the ground of all activities, imagination, and ideas. Only by caring for the soul can we humans find fulfillment and happiness. Nothing can be achieved in life if the soul is starving.

Taking care of the soul is to know yourself. Who am I? What is the meaning of my life? Why am I here on planet

Earth? What is my relationship with the world, with my friends, with my family, with my colleagues? All these questions are soul questions. We need time to ask these questions every day. We need time for contemplation and reflection. We need time to be ourselves. Time to be in relationship with others. The soul craves right relationships. The body is a vehicle for soul relationship. We embrace somebody with our body, but in truth it is the soul which embraces. If there is no soul, then there is no love, no friendship. Then our embrace is empty.

We need to feed our soul. As we feed our body with rice, vegetables, bread, and soup, we need to feed our soul with friendship, with love and compassion, with beauty and art, with singing and painting, with imagination and meditation, with silence and solitude. These are foods for the soul. If we don't feed our soul, we will suffer. Why is there so much depression, so many mental problems, frequent conflicts in relationships between husband and wife, between children and parents? All these breakdowns in relationship and mental problems are a consequence of not taking care of the soul. We take care of our bodies. We have big houses, big salaries, big cars, television sets and computers for our bodies—but we have no time for soul, no time for love, no time to meditate, no time for children. We spend so much of our attention and energy on having things that there is no time for being ourselves.

We feed the body three times a day. We worry about clothing the body. We work hard for hours and hours each day in order to house the body, but we spend very little time feeding and tending to the soul. The soul seeks happiness.

Through physical activities like dancing, walking, gardening, singing, cooking, and making things, we make ourselves happy. Through activities of the body, we reach the soul, thus body and soul support each other to find happiness.

We need to learn to be happy with ourselves. Happiness is our birthright. We should never allow anyone to steal our happiness from us. Let them steal our money, our car, our computer, but don't let them steal our happiness because happiness is the key to personal sustainability, which is as important as environmental sustainability. If we are not sustainable in our personal life, how can there be sustainability in the world?

The well-being of soil and soul must extend to the well-being of society. This is possible only when we organize our society on the principles of human dignity, equality, and social justice. How can it be right that some people own twenty thousand or fifty thousand acres of land, while others' lives are destitute? In Australia, some farmers have to go from one end of their land to the other in a helicopter because one farm can be as big as the state of Texas. This is not an order given us by Nature. It is an unjust order created by humans. Our social system has to be based on justice, sustainability, and spirituality. If we live in an unjust society, practicing spirituality in our personal lives is not easy.

The word *spirit* comes from *spiritus*—"breathing." Richard Dawkins, the scientist, once said to me, "Mr. Kumar, I don't believe in spirituality."

I answered, "Professor Dawkins, don't you believe in breathing?"

He said, "What do you mean?"

I said, "Spirituality means to breathe. You and I breathe together. That's spirituality. We are sharing a breath together. When we love our beloved, when we hold each other in our arms, we breathe together. We are all one. We are related to each other through breathing."

Life is sustained by breath. The moment we have that sense of shared breath, a sense of relationship to the world, we have spirituality. The great spiritual qualities of compassion, love, generosity, and service are practiced in loving relationships.

Spirituality can hardly exist in a mass society or in a corporate world where a person is a cog in a machine. How can we practice spirituality or have a relationship when we don't know our neighbors? In big cities like Paris, New York, Tokyo, or Mumbai, neighbors never meet, so how can they practice spirituality? In order to have meaningful relationships, we need small communities and we need to organize our society on a human scale. Although in the big cities, practice of spirituality is difficult, by developing a sense of neighborhoods, we may be able to create communities, take care of each other, and rise above isolated and individualized existence. Cities need to be redesigned and reformed into a network of neighborhoods.

Human-scale society is a spiritual imperative. Mahatma Gandhi advocated decentralized, local, small-scale village economies because in small-scale communities we can care for each other. We can have a relationship with each other. We can breathe together.

We have to create a social system which is equitable and just. At the moment, our society is designed in an unnatural way. Look at the natural world where animals, birds, and forests face no injustice. All animals from the smallest to the largest, from the mosquito and earthworm to the elephant and lion are fed, watered, and sheltered every day by the natural systems. Isn't that a marvelous system? Animals have no prime minister, no president, no chancellor of the Exchequer, no parliament, no prisons, no courts, and no wars. Theirs is a self-organizing, self-correcting, and self-managing natural system. A tiger in the forest and an earthworm in the soil are living together. The tiger never hurts the earthworm. Once a tiger has eaten, it does not hunt any animal. It will sleep. A deer will pass by and the tiger will not hurt it—a tiger will only hunt to feed itself, not to store food in the fridge. There is no greed in the community of tigers.

Then look at human society; it is not designed to make sure everyone is fed and sheltered. Millions of people go to bed without food, without shelter, and without water, while others waste food and own more clothes than they could ever wear. The rich keep houses empty while the poor are homeless.

We waste nearly 40 percent of food in Britain, according to a government analysis. In the supermarket, food which is past its sell-by date goes to a landfill, causing greenhouse gases. But supermarkets do not give this food to hungry people because it's illegal. That's the kind of legal system we have—it is legal to throw food away, but it is illegal to feed the hungry! Ours is a very unfair and unjust society. Our economic order is poorly designed. It perpetuates inequality and the exploitation of the weak. In a holistic vision for the twenty-first century, we need to redesign our economic, social, and political systems in such a way that nobody needs to be obese, nobody needs to be hungry, no food is wasted, and unused food is composted and returned to the earth. Waste should be made illegal.

The greatest curse of modern industrial society is waste. We take precious resources from Nature, extract them from mines, fields, and forests, turn them into consumable commodities, use them, and then throw them into a landfill. We have a linear economy, which is not Nature's economy. We have to learn from Nature. We have to create a circular economy. In Nature everything is cyclical. There is a cycle of time, there is a cycle of life. Everything in Nature is round. The sun is round, the moon is round, the Earth is round, trees are round. Our heads are round. The economy should also be cyclical. Everything we take from Nature should be used and then returned to Nature in a form which it can easily reabsorb. Then there is no waste. This is common sense, but unfortunately common sense is no longer common!

Holistic thinking brings soil, soul, and society together as three aspects of one big picture. This is the new trinity for our time. When we become single-issue oriented, we believe that if only the world could achieve environmental sustainability, or if only everyone could practice spirituality, or if only we could establish social justice in the world, then everything would be sorted. But this kind of single-issue obsession doesn't take us very far because it is too narrow. All issues are interrelated. The trinity of soil, soul, society encapsulates the big picture.

With this trinity in good balance, we can create a sustainable future for the whole of humanity and the whole of the Earth. Then humanity can survive not for a hundred years, not for a thousand years, but for millennia. This is possible if we humans tread lightly on the Earth and live a life of elegant simplicity within the context of soil, soul, and society.

There is nothing better than moderation.
The mark of moderate people is:
They are tolerant like the sky,
Firm like a mountain,
Supple like a tree in the wind.
They have no destination in view,
And make use of anything
Life happens to bring their way.

— LAO TZU

About the Author

SATISH KUMAR is long-time peace and environment activist and former monk who has been quietly setting the global agenda of change for over 50 years. He settled in the United Kingdom after an 8,000-mile peace pilgrimage and became editor of *Resurgence* magazine, a position he held from 1973–2016. During this time, he founded Devon's Schumacher College, authored several books, and presented the successful documentary *Earth Pilgrim*. He lives in Devon, UK.

Other Books by Satish Kumar

No Destination

You Are Therefore I Am

Spiritual Compass

Earth Pilgrim

The Buddha and the Terrorist

Soil, Soul, Society

A NOTE ABOUT THE PUBLISHER

New Society Publishers is an activist, solutions-oriented publisher focused on publishing books for a world of change. Our books offer tips, tools, and insights from leading experts in sustainable building, homesteading, climate change, environment, conscientious commerce, renewable energy, and more—positive solutions for troubled times.

We're proud to hold to the highest environmental and social standards of any publisher in North America. This is why some of our books might cost a little more. We think it's worth it!

- We print all our books in North America, never overseas

- All our books are printed on 100% **post-consumer recycled paper**, processed chlorine-free, with low-VOC vegetable-based inks (since 2002)

- Our corporate structure is an innovative employee shareholder agreement, so we're one-third employee-owned (since 2015)

- We're carbon-neutral (since 2006)

- We're certified as a B Corporation (since 2016)

At New Society Publishers, we care deeply about *what* we publish—but also about *how* we do business.

Download our catalog at https://newsociety.com/Our-Catalog or for a printed copy please email info@newsocietypub.com or call 1-800-567-6772 ext 111.

New Society Publishers
ENVIRONMENTAL BENEFITS STATEMENT

For every 5,000 books printed, New Society saves the following resources:[1]

21	Trees
1,911	Pounds of Solid Waste
2,103	Gallons of Water
2,742	Kilowatt Hours of Electricity
3,474	Pounds of Greenhouse Gases
15	Pounds of HAPs, VOCs, and AOX Combined
5	Cubic Yards of Landfill Space

[1]Environmental benefits are calculated based on research done by the Environmental Defense Fund and other members of the Paper Task Force who study the environmental impacts of the paper industry.